Beginning
Employment Law

Whether you're new to higher education, coming to legal study for the first time or just wondering what Employment Law is all about, **Beginning Employment Law** is the ideal introduction to help you hit the ground running. Starting with the basics and an overview of each topic, it will help you come to terms with the structure, themes and issues of the subject so that you can begin your Employment Law module with confidence.

Adopting a clear and simple approach with legal vocabulary explained in a detailed glossary, James Marson breaks the subject of Employment Law down using practical everyday examples to make it understandable for anyone, whatever their background. Diagrams and flowcharts simplify complex issues, important cases are identified and explained and on-the-spot questions help you recognise potential issues or debates within the law so that you can contribute in classes with confidence.

Beginning Employment Law is an ideal first introduction to the subject for LLB, GDL or ILEX students and especially international students, those enrolled on distance learning courses or on other degree programmes.

James Marson is Principal Lecturer in Law at Sheffield Hallam University.

Beginning the Law

A new introductory series designed to help you master the basics and progress with confidence.

Published in Spring 2014:

Beginning Employment Law, James Marson
Beginning Evidence, Charanjit Singh Landa
Beginning Human Rights, Howard Davis

Also available:

Beginning Constitutional Law, Nick Howard
Beginning Contract Law, Nicola Monaghan and Chris Monaghan
Beginning Criminal Law, Claudia Carr and Maureen Johnson
Beginning Equity and Trusts, Mohamed Ramjohn

www.routledge.com/cw/beginningthelaw

Beginning Employment Law

JAMES MARSON

Routledge
Taylor & Francis Group

LONDON AND NEW YORK

First published 2014
by Routledge
2 Park Square, Milton Park, Abingdon, Oxon OX14 4RN

and by Routledge
711 Third Avenue, New York, NY 10017

Routledge is an imprint of the Taylor & Francis Group, an informa business

British Library Cataloguing in Publication Data
A catalogue record for this book is available from the British Library

Library of Congress Cataloging in Publication Data
Marson, James.
Beginning employment law/James Marson.
  p. cm. – (Beginning the law)
  ISBN 978-0-415-65895-9 (hardback) – ISBN 978-0-415-65896-6 (pbk) –
  ISBN 978-1-315-81550-3 (ebk) 1. Labor laws and legislation–England.
  2. Labor laws and legislation–Wales. I. Title.
  KD3009.M255 2014
  344.4201–dc23   2013039180

ISBN: 978-0-415-65895-9 (hbk)
ISBN: 978-0-415-65896-6 (pbk)
ISBN: 978-1-315-81550-3 (ebk)

Typeset in Vectora
by Florence Production Ltd, Stoodleigh, Devon, UK

Printed and bound in Great Britain by
TJ International Ltd, Padstow, Cornwall

Contents

Table of Cases

Table of Legislation

Secondary legislation

Preface

Beginning Employment Law is an introduction to a remarkable jurisdiction of law. The topic is vast, it impacts on almost everyone's lives, and is continually changing, given the social, political and economic contexts in which it operates. Recent legislative action has further developed employment relations, has affected the availability to access legal rights, and the proposed changes to employment status, along with the continuing impact from the European Union, ensure employment law's status as a dynamic and topical subject for study.

This text assumes no prior knowledge of the subject. It begins by outlining the institutions that affect employment relations, including the tribunals and courts that hear employment disputes, the ever significant impact of the Advisory, Conciliation and Arbitration Service regarding codes of practice and practical assistance in all aspects of employment and labour law, and some of the international bodies that play a role in domestic employment law.

The main body of the text identifies the sources of the employment contract, the importance of the employment status of individuals, protection against discrimination and the obligations imposed on both employers and individuals in employment, the employer's obligation to pay wages, the common law and statutory provisions regarding termination of employment, and it concludes with an explanation of the law relating to maintaining industrial relations. Diagrams, tables and mind maps are used throughout the text in an attempt to make sense of the law, and to try to show how the various elements of the law work together. The companion website also contains a number of features to assist your learning and engagement with the subject.

Finally, I would like to offer my sincere thanks to my publishers at Routledge – Lloyd Langman who worked with me to begin the project, and to Damian Mitchell and Fiona Briden for their enthusiasm and patience with me in the development of the final draft. As ever, I would not have been able to complete this project without the love and support of Katy, Isabelle and Mia. They have always been my biggest supporters, always encourage me, and accept my time away from them while writing with humour and affection.

Any errors or omissions remain my own.

James Marson
August 2013

Guide to the Companion Website

www.routledge.com/cw/beginningthelaw

Visit the *Beginning the Law* website to discover a comprehensive range of resources designed to enhance your learning experience.

Answers to on-the-spot questions
Suggested answers from the author to the questions posed in the book.

Online glossary
Reinforce your legal vocabulary with our online glossary. You can find easy to remember definitions of all key terms, listed by chapter for each title in the *Beginning the Law* series.

Chapter 1
An introduction to the study of employment law

INTRODUCTION

Welcome to *Beginning Employment Law*. This book will introduce many of the most significant aspects of employment law and those which will undoubtedly feature in the syllabi of university courses offering an employment law module. It is written in the hope of giving you an accessible introduction to the most important issues in employment law, and that it will act as a springboard for you to go on and seek out materials to further your understanding of the many debates in this dynamic area of law.

THE TOPICS IN EMPLOYMENT LAW

The book begins the topic of employment law by identifying the key institutions involved in governing relations between the parties, and this applies at domestic and international levels. Then the details of the contract of employment, its sources and terms are identified before the text continues with a look at the first substantial issue, employment status. This is a matter of crucial significance as it acts as a gateway to many rights and obligations. Discrimination is then considered, along with pay in its widest sense and the requirement for equality of pay between men and women. The following three chapters deal with the other common reasons for employment disputes and claims to tribunals – terminations. Distinguishing between wrongful, unfair and constructive dismissal, and explaining the obligations imposed on employers when making employees redundant or when transferring a business are explained, as getting this area of law wrong can be very expensive to both parties to the relationship. The book concludes with an examination of industrial relations and the extent to which employees have power to bargain with the employer, and the employer's rights against trades unions in the event of industrial action.

UNIVERSITY STUDY: SELF-DIRECTED LEARNING

Modes of study at university vary depending on the subject being read, the institution, and the lecturer's teaching style (among other factors). However, it is common that a lecture to the student body, with corresponding seminars/tutorials, will be the model adopted. It is important to appreciate what each session is attempting to do.

Lectures

Lectures aim to give a broad overview of the substantive content of the subject. Depending on the content of the employment law module that you are studying, it is likely that you will have at least one or more sessions on, for example, employment status. The lecture will either give you a broad overview of the statutory and common law sources, highlighting the issues that you need to consider further before attending the seminar, or it may assume prior reading and identify key debates and nuances in the law for you to take into consideration when preparing for seminar discussions. Note that lectures are often a one-way system of delivery, with little interaction between the lecturer and audience.

Seminars

In seminars you have the opportunity to question colleagues and your tutor, to test ideas, and to practice your answers to essay-type or problem-based questions. They typically provide you with the ability to develop informed opinions, develop your research skills and ensure that you have found the most apt resources to enable you to apply legal rules, principles, and doctrine, and apply the law to problem situations, and develop your advocacy skills through debates, group discussions and presentations. These seminars, I would suggest, are where your real learning will take place. They provide continuous and immediate feedback. I recommend that you never lose sight of the fact that attendance at seminars, having fully prepared and engaged with the topic, will almost certainly guarantee you success in assessments. Many students are increasingly concerned with feedback and opportunities for constructive criticism to help them hone their skills and improve performance in assessments – seminars will provide all of these benefits.

One final point to make (I write this in the hope of not sounding patronising): the university has a responsibility to provide you with relevant instruction, the opportunity to engage with the staff and student body, and with materials to help you develop your understanding of the particular topic being studied. You also have a responsibility for your own learning as university education is founded upon self-directed learning. You will never get the full benefit of a seminar if you haven't tried to prepare as fully as possible. By reading the cases, by reading a textbook like this and then moving on to a more in-depth book, by reading journal articles, policy reports on so on, you will ensure that you can join in debates and understand what is being discussed in the seminars.

Don't worry if, having read cases in textbooks, you require greater help. I would suggest that if you find that there is anything you don't understand when reading – write a question and take it with you to the seminar. Seminar tutors will be very happy to assist you in your learning – that is what we are there for! By contrast, seminar tutors cannot provide the best help when a student attends a seminar and says 'I don't understand' without any further information. It is very difficult for a seminar tutor to provide any meaningful help because they have no point of reference about what the student has read and what has caused any misunderstanding or gaps in their knowledge. This is often where the negative perception of seminars is born. The seminar tutor, like a textbook, is a resource – use it.

FEEDBACK

Feedback is something everyone studying at university is looking for. It occupies a not insignificant amount of time for universities, particularly when considering the league table positions and student surveys, and, much more importantly, it is through feedback that you will have an opportunity to discover the extent of and limitations to your understanding and how you can positively improve your personal and professional development, and ability to succeed in assessments. There are, generally, two main forms of feedback that you will receive at university and it is important to understand what each seeks to achieve:

Formative feedback

Formative feedback is provided in the seminar by the tutors and by your colleagues. This is generally achieved through class discussions, and the feedback you will gain from the members of the seminar group will be informal and constructive. By attending seminars you will receive regular feedback, insofar as you actively engage and participate in the discussions, and it will help you identify techniques for presenting your arguments, using the information you have collated from textbooks, journals, case and statutory authority, and will certainly assist you in your development as an academic and a lawyer. Formative feedback is given to non-assessed contributions, and therefore will not be used directly to identify the grade you receive at the end of the module (sometimes referred to as a unit). However, I hope you will understand that this does not detract at all from the important function played by formative feedback and how it will be used in the summative feedback, which you will receive following the submission of assessed coursework/exams.

Summative feedback

Summative feedback is a very useful instrument to identify areas of good practice, clear understanding, evidence of effective research and incorporation of findings into your arguments, and, if done so constructively and taken in a positive frame of mind, it will point to areas of weakness and places where improvements could be made. Remember, even the most accomplished academic will seek critical reviews from colleagues in order to improve submissions to publishers and journal editors. You should not feel defensive about feedback, which identifies areas where you could have improved your arguments or used additional sources and so on. Some universities will use pre-prepared assessment feedback sheets, others will write commentary over your scripts; some academics will prepare a lengthy statement submitted on return of your script, whereas some will offer you an opportunity to receive oral feedback, but however the feedback is provided, it will be timely and detailed and should be used as a learning tool to help you improve. Ultimately, when you are answering a question on employment law, you will be judged primarily on your use of law, the sophistication of the analysis you have provided, clear evidence of research and understanding, and the persuasiveness of the arguments that you have presented – using materials which demonstrate evidence of wider reading.

KEY SOURCES AND LEARNING MATERIALS

There are various sources of information that are available to you when studying in higher education.

Module handbook

One of the first materials that you will be provided with, usually at the first lecture or in an induction programme, is the module manual or handbook. This will provide details of the topics to be included in your employment law module, the timetable, the lecture and seminar programme, an indicative reading list and links to sources in printed and electronic literature, and details of the virtual learning environment used by the institution together with materials that may be accessed from within. I would suggest that you read through this document thoroughly in order to understand the scope of the subject you are studying, the key areas that will be incorporated in your assessment, and other sources of information that will help when you begin employment law.

Reading lists

You will be provided with a reading list of key texts and commentaries that will assist your understanding of the topic. It is vitally important that you adopt the process of reading around a subject and not just relying on your own understanding, the views of your colleagues or those of your tutors and lecturers. The sources mentioned above are, of course, very important, and this is in no way diminishes the significance of what they will offer you in your development, but in order to provide a critical analysis of the law or of policy, and to ensure that you can fully develop your own thoughts on any particular topic, you need to expose yourself to as many views and commentaries as possible. The reading list provided will identify the specific case authorities, statutes and relevant sections, selected journal articles and chapters from textbooks, and it will also identify those that are compulsory, those that are recommended, and those that are part of wider reading. It is unlikely that you will be able to read everything on these lists, but if you work collaboratively with your colleagues in the seminar group, you can share the reading between each other and thereby ensure that all the material is covered and everyone engages in the seminar having been influenced by the materials that have been read.

Libraries/learning centres

The library, although increasingly it is being called a 'learning centre' or something similar, is a resource which, by the time you come to study employment law, should be very familiar to you. This is the place where you will find physical and electronic resources and audio and visual equipment so that you can view recordings of television and radio programmes. Obviously it is the place where you can loan books, and it is where experts in the profession (librarians) are located to help you with your legal research. It is also a venue where you will find space for individual private study, silent study, and group activities via bookable study areas. You can also request books and materials not available from your library through document supply resources and inter-library loan schemes.

Textbooks and statute books

You will be provided with details about the compulsory, recommended, and wider reading textbooks that will be used for your particular module. There are many textbooks on employment law available, each with their own focus (being practical, theory-based, cases and materials etc.) or unique selling point, and therefore there is little point in me providing you with a list. The module handbook, the lecture, and your module leader will inform you of this list and this will direct your reading. There are also several producers of statute books and it is worthwhile purchasing (if you can) one of these books and having it with you whenever you are in your class. Employment law is heavily legislated and while the common law principles and cases are vitally important, many updates in the law come through legislation and it is important to source and correctly cite the law. The statute books available include:

- Kidner, R. (ed.) (2013) *Blackstone's Statutes on Employment Law 2013–14*, Oxford University Press.
- Wallington, P. (2012) *Butterworth's Employment Law Handbook 2013*, LexisNexis Butterworths.
- Lauterburg, D. (2013) *Core Statutes on Employment Law 2013–14*, Palgrave Macmillan.

Journals

A very important source of information, and one that you should become familiar with immediately, is the articles produced in journals. There are general academic journals, among the best of which is *Modern Law Review* and *Law Quarterly Review*. Further, there are specialist employment journals, such as the *Industrial Law Journal*, the *Industrial Relations Journal*, and the *British Journal of Industrial Relations*, which should be regularly consulted for commentary and analysis on contemporary issues and developments in the law. Finally, there are practitioner-based publications such as the *Solicitors Journal* and the *New Law Journal*, which contain shorter pieces, but are often more contemporary as they are published with greater frequency then those others identified in this section.

Virtual learning environment

There are several virtual learning environment (VLE) providers used by universities throughout the world. The specific VLE used by your institution is somewhat irrelevant, the important factor is that you access the materials and understand its purpose. Do not see the VLE as an electronic repository or noticeboard. It is far more sophisticated and beneficial to your learning than that. It will contain materials such as an electronic copy of the module handbook, lecture slides, seminar materials, links to electronic sources, and so on. But, it is also the place where virtual group discussions can take place, communication with tutors and collaborations on group work is made accessible – far easier than having to meet up in person. Therefore, make sure that you use the technology and understand all the benefits that it may provide to assist you in your learning and development.

Online databases

You will already be quite familiar with legal research, studying methods, and you will be experienced in producing material for assessed coursework and exams. However, in my experience it is never a wasted opportunity to remind students of the substantial material that is available in online databases, and to encourage you to get into the habit of regularly using these as part of your research. Most universities will be subscribers to Westlaw, LexisNexis, Lawtel or any number of repositories for legal materials. Case law, statutes, newspaper reports, theses, journal articles, policy reports, and so on, are now available electronically. You may have to access these materials through the university's intranet, but increasingly they are made available through your personal computer, tablet, or smartphone. Ensure that you are fully aware of the databases available and use them! Legal research is far easier than it used to be when these materials were held physically in libraries, and therefore you can spend your time reading, rather than locating, this information. Also be aware that most university libraries or learning centres have dedicated staff to assist you with your research, and this may be particularly useful if you decide to undertake a dissertation module or postgraduate research study.

Electronic sources

Increasingly information is being made available electronically. Having access to databases, websites and search engines ensures that you can use these materials (through university portals at least) relatively easily. The following list identifies some of the sources that I think would be of value to you in your research and wider reading. This is by no means an exhaustive list, and guidance will be provided by the lecturer, but it is useful and will certainly help you in gaining a broad perspective of employment law and employment issues:

- Legislation Direct: this resource has the full text of all statutes and statutory instruments in force.
- Westlaw, contains (among others) the full text of domestic and European Union (EU) legislation and case law.
- Lawtel LexisNexis: Lexis Library Employment Law Online – contains case reports from the Industrial Relations Law Reports (IRLR) and the practitioner encyclopaedia Harvey.
- Advisory, Conciliation and Arbitration Service (ACAS) (www.acas.org.uk): this website contains very useful information regarding codes of practice used in tribunals, interactive guides and resources for employers and individuals.
- The Department for Business, Innovation and Skills (www.bis.gov.uk/): DBIS is the government department responsible for employment law and contains access to materials and consultation documents relating to the broad subject of employment relations.
- The EU Commission website on employment matters (http://europa.eu.int/comm/employment_social/labour_law/index).
- The website of the European Court of Human Rights (ECHR) (www.echr.coe.int): this site details case law, statistics and official documents.
- A website run by a barrister specialising in employment law (http://daniel barnett.co.uk): Daniel Barnett provides a truly excellent website and free mailing list, which contains updates in the law and is a resource any student/practitioner of English and EU employment law should be accessing.
- Details of the courts and tribunals in England and Wales (www.justice.gov.uk/about/hmcts/index.htm).

HOW TO ANSWER EMPLOYMENT QUESTIONS

Modes of assessment vary between universities. The way you are assessed for your employment law module could include coursework in the form of writing a essay, or answering a problem-based question. It may also require you to present orally an answer to a question, you could be assessed through seminar contributions, or you may be asked to present a written answer to a question and then complete a viva. Regardless of the way in which you are assessed, and in whatever form your module leader wishes you to answer and present your work, there are some underlying features which will be present regardless of the assessment instrument or the requirements of the institution and lecturer.

Before you begin, you should familiarise yourself with the assessment instrument, the guide to referencing and citations used in the department in which you are studying, and if in any doubt as to how to present your answer, ask the module leader for guidance and/or obtain a text on referencing law essays and exams.

It is very likely that the module handbook will contain a descriptive account of the module, its aims and, very importantly, the assessment criteria linked with the learning outcomes. This material will also be used by the teaching staff to guide their marking. For example, I might identify assessment criteria to include evidence of reading and research, identification of legal issues, identification and use of legal principles and doctrines, the clarity and accuracy of the use of materials and their incorporation into a persuasive argument and/or suggested solution. By providing the student with this information, the student immediately understands the nature of what I am looking for when marking their script. There is no guesswork involved: the student needs to understand the question, clearly identify the critical legal issues that require an answer, to have undertaken effective and comprehensive research into those areas, to have used all available materials in assisting an answer and grounding arguments, and have disseminated this information in a clear and grammatically correct way. Students who obtain the highest marks will have provided evidence in each of these categories.

Therefore, a method that you may like to adopt (having consulted with your lecturer before beginning) has the following components.

Reading the question

This is an obvious point but one which is sometimes missed, particularly in a stressful situation such as an examination. You will not be asked to write everything you know about a particular topic. Rather, you will be asked to critique a point of law, comment on new developments in case law or legislation, or advise parties in a practical scenario (for example). Therefore, ensure that you read the question thoroughly and that you understand exactly what the examiner is looking for from your answer. This will assist you in the next stage, which is to begin your research (when answering coursework questions – in an examination, the research will already have been completed).

Beginning your research

Research should begin at the earliest opportunity. Do not wait until the last moment to begin your research or to write up your answer. Technological problems occur as a very common feature of university life. It is also, sadly, quite commonplace that such problems occur at the most inopportune times. Further, be aware that many universities do not accept lost data, problems with printers, etc. as (acceptable) reasons to provide extensions for late submission of work. Also, ensure that you keep an accurate bibliography or references list (there are several computer-based applications available to help with this process), which will demonstrate wider reading and also avoid any problems with plagiarism.

Reading around the subject with purpose

It is very difficult to attempt to read everything on employment law because the subject is so large that in any university module you will not study employment law, but rather select individual elements (albeit very important and fundamental elements) of the subject. As such, having identified the question and understood the nature of what is being required from you, you should consult the relevant materials including cases, statutes, journal articles, policy papers, and other specialist literature. You also need to understand what is significant about what you have read and how it can be incorporated into your answer to ground your argument. By this I mean you justify your answer on the basis of legal/academic commentary and/or case law/statutory authority. I would also avoid reading too many textbooks. There is only so much information any textbook can provide, even with the author's own commentary on the subject. Rather, to obtain the higher grades you will need to consult journal articles and use judgments from appropriate cases to demonstrate your understanding and knowledge. Reading around a subject, and using the evidence found, will provide you with a better opportunity to demonstrate a critical analysis or critical application of the law. The 'critical' dimension is what will separate grades in the higher categories, from those descriptive answers which will generally be awarded a lower grade.

Making notes while you read

One of the key skills to be developed is for you to be able to present the ideas produced by another, but in your own words. Direct quotes are often useful, but it is also important for you to be able to demonstrate what other academics and lawyers have said about a particular issue. This is easier when you have made your notes while reading and while the information is fresh in your memory. You will also be able to demonstrate your understanding better by being able to explain a particular law or a particular journal article if you can do so in your own words.

Writing

Having read the question, identified the legal issues, researched the area thoroughly and with purpose, and having made appropriate notes, you are in a position to begin writing your answer. This is an aspect of completing assessed coursework that should be done within a comfortable time frame so that you do not suffer adversely when (for example) technological problems or other issues occur, resulting in you missing the deadline for submission of work. Universities, as I have previously stated, work to strict rules and while there may be some limited discretion available, committees are usually the objective bodies that determine whether an extension should be provided or a student's reason for late or non-submission of work should be accepted. Do not put yourself in this position if it can be avoided.

Your answer to a piece of coursework, as it would be in an exam, should include an introduction whereby you identify the legal issues and briefly state the laws that you are going to use to answer the question. This will immediately signal to the examiner that you are aware of the relevant points and give the examiner confidence that your answer will contain relevant materials. In the main body of your answer you should focus on the most significant legal issues and use your legal research in providing an answer with authority. Employment law often contains competing theories or, for example, in employment status questions, there may be competing authorities to be included. It is the detailed research, ability to articulate your argument with brevity, and your clear identification of an answer underpinned by authority that will provide a convincing answer.

Submitting your work

It is always appropriate to read through the draft of your work to ensure the arguments and points made flow and are easy to understand, and that your use of language and grammar is correct. It is quite easy to feel that this will be a waste of your time having completed the work, but as lecturers are often only allowed to grade your work on the basis of your submission (unless you will be assessed through seminar contributions or some other similar instrument), it is very valuable to re-read your work to ensure it is as meaningful as you intended. When you do submit your work, be aware of the location and time of the particular deadline. There may be traffic problems, technological problems, or you may face some personal situation that could affect your ability to submit on time. This latter example will usually allow you an excuse for late submission, but the others generally won't. Do not leave submission to the very last moment as this can often end in upset and the imposition of unnecessary sanctions.

CONCLUSION

This introductory chapter is designed to identify some key criteria to be used in your study. Employment law is an area in continual development, both domestically and internationally, and as such you must use the materials identified above to ensure you keep aware of changes in the law, readily identify the consultation processes through which you can be involved in the development of laws impacting on employment relations, and understand the major institutions affecting the parties and their relation to each other and third parties.

The book begins now with the first of the substantive employment chapters – the institutions affecting employment law.

Chapter 2
Institutions in employment relations

LEARNING OBJECTIVES

After reading this chapter you should be able to:

- identify the main institutions governing employment dispute resolution in England and Wales;
- explain the role played by ACAS in promoting good industrial relations;
- explain the process of a dispute, through initial resolution attempts to a case being heard in the tribunals/courts;
- identify key changes in the fees and costs awarded in employment disputes.

MIND MAP

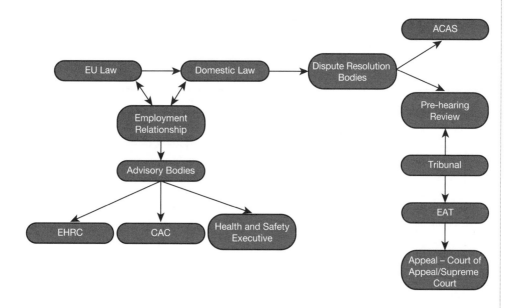

INTRODUCTION

Employment law is a very broad concept. It can involve almost any aspect of an employment relationship, from when an employer first decides to advertise for staff to assist with his/her business, dealing with the operation of the relationship, liaising with collective bargaining bodies, trade unions, and government agencies who will affect the relationship, to the eventual termination of the relationship either by the employer or the individual.

Key Definition: Common law

While many employment laws are established through statute (such as the Employment Rights Act 1996), there are also rights and obligations governed by the common law. It is law created through judicial decisions and is a body of law developed before a united system of government had been formed in England.

Key Definition: Statute/statutory

A statute refers to an act of the legislature and may be referred to as an 'Act of parliament'/'legislation'.

Key Definition: Employee

An individual engaged under a 'contract of service'. Employees enjoy the greatest employment protections and rights, although they have greater obligations imposed on them (in part through many implied terms).

Employment law, then, has to consider both the internal and external elements affecting the relationship. There will be an agreement between the individual and the employer, which is underpinned by the contract of employment. This is subject to numerous sources, some of which are decided by the parties (although in reality for most individuals this is largely determined by the employer), and others which are imposed on the parties either through the **common law**, customs, or statute. These constitute the express and implied terms that are applicable to the employment relationship. It is crucial for your knowledge of employment law, that you are aware of the sources and can identify the extent to which they impose obligations and provide rights to both parties.

It is also important to be aware of the effect of trade union membership and collective bargaining in determining the regulation of the employment relationship.

DISPUTE RESOLUTION BODIES

It is inevitable that in an employment relationship there will be disputes between the parties. This could involve the health and safety of individuals at work, it may involve arguments about pay and working conditions, it may involve issues regarding harassment, stress and bullying at work, and it may also involve an employer's re-organisation of the workplace, or indeed an employer's decision to terminate the contract of any or all of the individuals engaged. Where there is such a dispute, this may involve individual employment rights (for example, the right not to be unfairly dismissed or unfairly selected for redundancy) and/or it may involve collective employment rights (for example, trade union membership or the application of disciplinary procedures). To resolve these disputes, there are a number of bodies that have been established in order to promote good industrial relations and to resolve disputes in as amicable a manner as is possible.

Key Definition: Unfair dismissal

This is a statutory-based right protecting employees against certain types of dismissal. An employer must identify a potentially fair reason for dismissal and use the appropriate procedure to ensure a dismissal is considered fair.

Key Definition: Alternative forms of dispute resolution

These have been developed in an attempt to settle disputes between parties without the issue having to be settled by a court or tribunal.

The main dispute resolution bodies in employment law are identified below. For most individuals seeking to resolve a problem, it may seem natural to begin with the **employment tribunal**. The employment tribunal, for want of a better analogy, is an employment court. It is the forum to which **employees** will bring their cases when in dispute with an employer. It is important to recognise the role of the Advisory,

Key Definition: Employment tribunal

Employment tribunals (previously called Industrial Tribunals) hear and resolve employment disputes (dismissals; discrimination; cases involving other statutory rights and some common law ones). They are presided over by an Employment Judge who can be assisted by two wing members representing (generally, rather than specific to the case) both employers and workers.

Key Definition: ACAS

The Advisory, Conciliation and Arbitration Service is a body established under the Employment Protection Act 1975 to resolve disputes between parties in an employment relationship, provide free advice, promote good industrial relations, and to establish Codes of Practice such as that used in cases of disciplinary and dismissal matters (Code of Practice 1– Disciplinary and Grievance Procedures).

Conciliation and Arbitration Service (**ACAS**). ACAS was established to facilitate the amicable resolution of employment disputes. It follows from a general movement to **alternative forms of dispute resolution** which is included in all civil cases. Where employment disputes cannot be resolved through conciliation or arbitration, they will proceed to an employment tribunal, but, as with all civil cases, it is important to consider the non-court resolution techniques prior to going to litigation.

The role of ACAS

ACAS was established in 1975 following a series of increasing tensions between employers and individuals represented by trade unions. The 1970s and 1980s are noted in the history of England and Wales as being a time of employment disputes on a national scale and an increasingly militant trade union movement. This was disruptive to the UK economy and it was deemed by the Labour government that action was needed to help resolve the sources of disputes. Since 1975, ACAS has provided an invaluable service, assisting employers and trades unions to resolve disputes without, necessarily, recourse to industrial action or to resolving the problem in an employment tribunal. Arbitration and conciliated settlements are the priorities for ACAS.

It is also important to recognise that ACAS is also a source of information, guidance and training for the parties involved in employment relationships. They provide interpretation of legislation and practical guidance to assist parties in understanding their rights and obligations. Further, a crucial role of ACAS has been in the development of the ACAS Code of Practice on Disciplinary and Grievance Procedures (among other codes of practice). Tribunals will refer to this Code of Practice when assessing the reasonableness of an employer's decision to discipline or dismiss an individual. While not law, tribunals will seek an explanation from employers if the employer has not adhered to the Code's content. It is therefore very significant in relation to **unfair dismissal** and redundancy law.

Case management

Pre-hearing reviews

In line with general civil case management, there has been a movement towards the use of pre-hearing reviews before cases reach an employment tribunal. This may be initiated by the Employment Judge, or it may be requested by one of the parties. The principle behind a pre-hearing review is to determine the legal issues which have to be raised in the case, the use and availability of witnesses, and clarification of any potentially complex areas of law, particularly in the case of discrimination and equal pay claims.

Another reason for a pre-hearing review is to determine potential awards of costs where there is little chance of success of the claimant's argument, or where the Employment Judge considers that the case should be struck out as (1) it has no reasonable prospect of success, or is (2) vexatious or (3) scandalous. The judge may also advise a claimant who wishes to pursue a case under one of the three heads identified above, that an award of legal costs may be imposed which, following the Employment Tribunals (Constitution and Rules of Procedure) (Amendment) Regulations 2012, SI 2012/468, can amount to a maximum of £20,000. Under Rule 41(2) of the Employment Tribunal Rules of Procedure, a tribunal must have regard to a party's ability to pay when determining costs. But note that in *Shields Automotive Ltd v Ronald Greig* [2011] UKEATS/0024/10/BI the **Employment Appeal Tribunal** (EAT) held that capital assets (such as the individual's house) should form part of this assessment.

Key Definition: Employment Appeal Tribunal

This is not a tribunal (despite its name) but is the court that hears cases of appeals from employment tribunals.

Employment tribunals

Employment tribunals, previously known as industrial tribunals, were initially established to hear claims of unfair dismissal by employees. This right had been given to employees through the Industrial Relations Act 1971. Since then, there has been a vast increase in the jurisdiction of employment law and related issues. Unfair dismissal, redundancy, minimum wage, working time regulations, discrimination, harassment, victimisation, transfer of an undertaking, equal pay. This is just a very short list of the issues now heard by employment tribunals. The concept of tribunals being a quick, cheap and informal mechanism to resolve employment disputes has essentially vanished. They are very technical and legalistic in their approach, bound as they are by statutory procedures and codes of practice. Simplifying employment law has been a desire of many governments, yet in almost every case, attempts to simplify employment relations merely lead to greater regulation and complexity. This is not a particularly favoured outcome for either party to a dispute.

Where the parties to an employment dispute cannot resolve their differences through a form of alternative dispute resolution, the dispute will be heard in an employment tribunal. Employment disputes between an employer and employee based on statutory rights are heard in this forum. Claims of breach of contract are generally heard in the ordinary civil courts. So too are cases where individuals are claiming wrongful dismissal (a common law claim against the wrongful termination of the contract of employment). However, where the claim of damages is less than £25,000, it will also be heard in an employment tribunal.

Composition

Tribunals get their name from the three members who make up the panel deciding the case. The composition of the tribunal is the chair and two lay/wing members. The chair is a person with specialist knowledge of employment law, known as an Employment Judge, and the wing members are individuals who, broadly, represent the interests of the employer and employee. For example, the wing member representing the employers' side would be selected from a body such as the Confederation of British Industry. The wing member representing the employees' side would be selected from a body such as the Trades Union Congress. Remember, however, these are independent appointments and these representatives are not there to argue the case for the employer or employee. While the Employment Judge is an expert in the law, the wing members present assist the judge in offering some practical and business insight into the particular scenario presented to the tribunal. This structure has been referred to as an 'industrial jury.'

This element of the industrial jury system has an important dimension to it. It is not uncommon for the Employment Judge to come to a decision that is different from the decision made by the two wing members. In such a situation, the Employment Judge is outvoted and the decision of the majority is taken to produce the award of the tribunal. This demonstrates the equal status of each member of the tribunal and the significant role each plays in a tribunal award.

Employment Judges have been able to sit alone to hear cases involving an employer failing in his/her duty to provide an employee with the written statement of employment particulars (as required under s. 1 Employment Rights Act (ERA) 1996). They may also hear cases without wing members where a trade union is seeking compensation for an employer's breach of consultation requirements in relation to redundancies. Most recently, and most controversially, the ability for an Employment Judge to sit alone has been extended to cases of unfair dismissal. Cases involving allegations of discrimination are heard by a three-member panel.

Employment tribunal statistics

Statistics published by the Ministry of Justice for the period 2011–12 identified that there was a 15 per cent fall in the number of claims received from 2010–11 and a 21 per cent fall in claims compared with those received in 2009–10.

Of the claims received in 2011–12, 31 per cent were for unfair dismissal, breach of contract and redundancy; 29 per cent were concerning working time regulations, and 16 per cent were for unauthorised deductions (Wages Act 1986) (see Table 2.1 for examples of the successes of claims in these areas).

Table 2.1 Breakdown of claims and their resolution

Claims accepted	Withdrawn (%)	ACAS (%)	Struck out (%)	Successful at hearing (%)
Unfair dismissal – 46,300	24	42	9	8
Equal pay – 28,800	44	37	19	Less than 1
Working time regulations – 94,700	23	32	9	17

The above figures in Table 2.1, while painting a somewhat depressing picture of the success of those individuals claiming to have been unfairly dismissed or a victim of unequal pay, does at least show the significant role played by ACAS in resolving disputes without having to go to tribunal.

TRIBUNALS AND JUDGES SITTING ALONE

As part of the government's attempt to change the tribunal system to make it fairer to all parties, and in an attempt to reduce costs associated with dismissals (part of its 'austerity measures'), the Employment Tribunals Act 1996 (Tribunal Composition) Order 2012 SI 2012/988 came into effect on 6 April 2012. It allowed for Employment Judges to sit alone when hearing unfair dismissal cases rather than to have the lay/wing members hear the case and draw upon, what Lady Smith in *McCafferty v Royal Mail* [2012] UKEATS/0002/12/BI considered was their 'valuable common sense'. In that case, the judge was in the minority (as having substituted her own views for that of the employer), but clearly, the case being heard by a tribunal led to the claimant being held not to have been unfairly dismissed. Had the same case been heard under the new procedures by the same judge sitting alone, the decision would have been one of unfair dismissal (though this would likely have been changed following a subsequent appeal). The consequence is that when using these new procedures, the parties and their representatives should look very closely at the reasoning for the decision of the Employment Judge and consider the issue and value of the so-called 'industrial jury' (see *Williams v Compair Maxam Ltd* [1982] ICR 156).

PRESENTATION OF A CLAIM

Claims by an employee to be heard at an employment tribunal begin with the employee completing a form known as an ET1 form and submitting this either to the tribunal office or through the employment tribunal service website. The form identifies details of the employee's claim against the employer and should be completed in as detailed manner as possible, as the information articulated in the form will be the basis of the claim (and any evaluation of its likely success at a pre-hearing review).

An employer will likely respond to the claim of the employee by completing an ET3 form. This must be completed within 28 days of the employer receiving the employee's ET1 form. Where an employer fails to answer the ET1 form through a return of the ET3 they will be barred from participating in any proceedings to determine whether the employee's claim should succeed.

The claim by an employee must also be lodged at a tribunal within the relevant time limits. The relevant **statute** identifies the time limit applicable to each 'right' (the source of the claim) and as such, tribunals have very limited discretion to extend time periods. In relation to claims of discrimination applicable to the Equality Act (EA) 2010, s. 123 provides the power for tribunals to hear cases presented outside the relevant time limit where the tribunal considers it 'just and equitable' to do so. Under s. 111(2) ERA 1996, an employment tribunal has the power to consider a case presented outside of the relevant time limit, but only where it is satisfied that it was not 'reasonably practicable' for the claimant to have lodged a claim within the time. Tribunals are very strict in this interpretation and they will not extend the time period simply because the individual was unaware of the law, he/she mismanaged their time, or was given erroneous advice by their adviser or trade union (for example). One exception to this general rule has been where erroneous advice was provided by a member of the tribunal service. In the case *Jean Sorelle Ltd v Rybak* [1991] IRLR 153, the tribunal extended the period for presentation of the claim due to a member of the tribunal's staff informing a claimant that weekends were not included in the calculation of the three-month period for lodging an unfair dismissal claim.

REPRESENTATION AT AN EMPLOYMENT TRIBUNAL

As employment tribunals are becoming increasingly complex in the procedures under which they operate, and technical rules must be complied with – particularly in relation to discrimination and equal pay claims – those who bring claims and those who proceed to a hearing at a tribunal are at a disadvantage when not represented (particularly if not 'legally' represented). The disadvantage is compounded when an employer, against whom the individual is claiming, is represented (and frequently this is by a lawyer). The limitation in obtaining financial assistance in preparing a claim can disadvantage claimant employees/workers. Recent trends have been to reduce funding for advisory services offered by bodies such as Citizens Advice (often the source of legal rights to individuals). Further, qualitative research from 2001, 2002 and 2005 has demonstrated the difficulty many individuals have in accessing not-for-profit advisory services. Given the procedural nature of legal action through an employment tribunal, difficulty in accessing advice, information and representation impacts negatively on many (especially poorer) individual's opportunities to seek redress. Further, when individuals claim they have been unfairly dismissed/unfairly selected for redundancy, etc. they often suffer from the 'cluster effect' of problems associated with loss of income and problems obtaining alternative work – e.g. welfare benefits, housing and debt. The problems facing individuals who want to have their case heard should not be underestimated.

Definitive figures are difficult to obtain due to the problems in gathering and collating the information. The data provided in 2011–12, collated by the Ministry of Justice, identified that 159,000 respondent claimants had been represented in tribunal proceedings, and of those, 72,600 identified that they had been represented by a solicitor, a Law Centre or a Trade Association. In the same time period, 321,800 claims were accepted by employment tribunals.

Employment Appeal Tribunal

The Employment Appeal Tribunal (EAT) is the body that hears appeals from employment tribunal awards. Despite its name, it is actually part of the High Court. Appeals to the EAT may be made by either party, but, like many appeals in the civil jurisdiction, it must be made on a point of law. It is very difficult to appeal against an award of an employment tribunal on the facts or simply because one party disagreed with that of the tribunal. The other method of successfully appealing is where an employment tribunal has reached a decision that is 'perverse'. This simply means it was an award that no reasonable tribunal would have made.

It is interesting to note that the EAT will not readily overturn an award made by an employment tribunal where the tribunal has correctly applied the law and the award made was not perverse. Employment tribunals make decisions/awards on the basis of a 'mix of law and fact'. The law element is quite straightforward in that it is the correct interpretation and application of the relevant laws. The fact element is much more complicated. Take for example a very topical issue in employment law – the employment status of an individual. Employment status is a gateway to many protective rights and it is not infrequently contested between the employer and individual. A university lecturer may very well be an employee, but so may be a surgeon, refuse collector, professional footballer, etc. Each will have distinct elements to their job, and will naturally involve very different responsibilities and working relationships with their employer. Therefore, the facts of a case will have a significant impact on the decision reached by a tribunal. As such, be very careful when you begin reading case reports (this is the common law/case law) to correctly identify legal principles (which will apply to future cases) from fact specific decisions (which by their nature will only apply to the facts heard by the tribunal in that particular case). In this second example, such a decision will not establish a general principle of law.

The previous paragraph was included simply to note the fact that different tribunals may very well come to different conclusions about the same case. This is no different to the EAT. Indeed, in the case *Woods v WM Car Services Ltd* [1982] ICR 693, the EAT dismissed an appeal by the employee even though it remarked that had it heard the case, the EAT would have decided differently from the tribunal. However, as there was no error of law and the decision of the tribunal was not perverse, the EAT had no choice but to dismiss the appeal.

Where there has been an error of law, the EAT will change the award made by the tribunal. However, where there has been a decision made by a tribunal on the facts, which has led to a perverse decision, the EAT will not substitute its view for that of the original tribunal, rather the case will be remitted back to the same or a differently constituted tribunal to hear the case again.

Subsequent appeals to the Court of Appeal/ the Supreme Court

Following the hierarchy of courts in England and Wales, appeals from the EAT will be heard in either the Court of Appeal or the **Supreme Court**. It is worth noting at this stage that the judicial function of the House of Lords was replaced in October 2009 by the Supreme Court. When you read appeal cases in employment law, you may still read about judgments of the House of Lords. This is simply because most of the important cases will have been heard by the House of Lords. New cases will be heard by the Supreme Court, and reference to the House of Lords and the Supreme Court is essentially to the same body. This is the highest court in England and Wales.

Appeals to the Court of Appeal will only be made on points of law, not on the facts of the case. As the Supreme Court hears cases of appeal of 'general significance,' relatively few employment cases will go that far. They will be heard by the Court of Appeal. Those cases that are heard by the Court of Appeal/the Supreme Court in employment law, are usually cases dealing with discrimination.

Key Definition: Supreme Court

The highest court of appeal in England and Wales. While the Court of Appeal hears many appeals (from lower courts), the Supreme Court hears appeals of general significance.

BINDING FORCE OF PRECEDENT

Precedent is the doctrine through which lower courts are bound by the decisions of higher courts. As such, judgments of the Supreme Court are binding on all lower courts and the employment tribunal. Note however, judgments of the Supreme Court do not bind the Supreme Court and the Supreme Court may choose to make a different decision on the same legal point in a future case. Likewise with the EAT, decisions are not binding on future cases heard by the EAT, but they are binding on employment tribunals. Finally, awards made by employment tribunals do not establish precedent as there is no court or tribunal below an employment tribunal in the hierarchy of the court system. This is perhaps one of the main reasons for the seemingly inconsistent decisions/awards made in employment tribunals.

CHANGES TO FEE STRUCTURE

In recent years some people in industry have held the view that unfair dismissal legislation, in particular, was unfair to employers who found it time consuming and potentially costly to dismiss an employee – where they had a right to do so. The issue raised at the time was about qualifying employees bringing a claim that they had been unfairly dismissed with no requirements to pay to have the case heard. This meant that many employees brought unsubstantiated claims, claims which generally would have had little chance of success of winning an unfair dismissal claim, although there was very little that either the employer or tribunal could do to stop many proceeding. Given this scenario, an employer would still have to gather information, allow staff time to complete forms, attend tribunals as witnesses and so on. This increase in bureaucracy, the government claimed, was preventing some employers from choosing to hire staff.

The government, underpinned by its austerity measures, has introduced the following changes to employment protection (applicable since 29 July 2013, although at the time of writing the introduction of fees is subject to judicial review). It is arguable whether they are particularly onerous to employees or simply a measure to increase fairness between an employer and employee.

The requirement of submitting an initial fee to pursue a claim in an employment tribunal is to ensure that claimants who use the tribunal service contribute to the running of the system. It was, argued the government, unfair to require taxpayers to pay all of this bill. It may also be an 'encouragement' for claimants to use alternative forms of dispute resolution before deciding to take the case to a tribunal.

There are two levels of fees (depending on the complexity of the case and how long it will take to be determined):

> Type A claims: an Issue fee of £160 and a Hearing fee of £230; and
> Type B claims: an Issue fee of £250 and a Hearing fee of £950.

Examples of Type A claims include holiday pay, unlawful deduction from wages, and so on. Examples of Type B claims include unfair dismissal and discrimination. All claims submitted to the EAT involve an Issue fee of £400 and a Hearing fee of £1,200.

On-the-spot question

The above fees would have a very negative effect on the poorest in society if introduced without a system of remission. The current system used in the civil courts, where the fees can be waived for those without the resources to pay, applies to these costs in both the employment tribunal and the EAT. Is that sufficient to prevent potential claimants from pursuing their rights through tribunals?

ADVISORY BODIES

Central arbitration committee

The role of the Central Arbitration Committee (CAC) is primarily to regulate industrial relations between employers and employees. This may involve arbitration in disputes between the parties, it also may be used to determine an employer's requirement to recognise a trade union, and it has functions in relation to collective bargaining agreements and their enforcement.

The Equality and Human Rights Commission

The Commission (EHRC) was established through EA 2006 to bring together the three separate commissions relating to discrimination law – the Equal Opportunities Commission, the Commission for Racial Equality, and the Disability Rights Commission. The jurisdiction of the Commission is to promote awareness of, and to positively end all forms of unlawful discrimination, be they based on sex, race, disability, sexual orientation, or age.

The Commission was created to promote equality and positive reinforcement and practices in relation to anti-discrimination and human rights. It provides guidance and codes of practice – albeit its remit is much broader than simply employment relations – to ensure that employers comply with the law and to promote equality of opportunity. It further has the power to issue an Unlawful Act Notice (enforced by the County Court) where an individual has been subject to an unlawful act of discrimination or violation of his/her human rights. The Commission also provides guidance for employers and employees on rights and responsibilities in relation to EA 2010 (this is achieved through its Code of Practice on EA).

Finally, the Commission is tasked with monitoring the UK's compliance with the European Convention on Human Rights (implemented through the Human Rights Act 1998). The European Convention must be taken into account by employers and is an increasing source of litigation, such as the recent *Eweida* case regarding the right to manifest a religious belief under Article 9 of the Convention (*Eweida & Others v UK* [2013] (Applications nos. 48420/10, 59842/10, 51671/10 and 36516/10)).

Health and Safety Executive

The Health and Safety Executive (HSE) is the body established as a watchdog for work-related health, safety and occupational illness matters. It operates through the Health and Safety at Work etc. Act 1974, which is the primary legislation for occupational health and safety in Great Britain, and various statutory instruments (secondary legislation), and is tasked (with other bodies) with enforcing the law. Beyond enforcement, the HSE also produces research and statistics to inform employers and employers of potential workplace dangers and methods of avoidance.

The HSE will be called in to investigate serious accidents at work, occupational diseases and specified dangerous occurrences. The Reporting of Injuries, Diseases and Dangerous Occurrences Regulations 1995 impose an obligation on employers, self-employed persons and people in charge of work premises to report such occurrences to the HSE. However, recent changes (as of April 2013) have meant that low-risk businesses will only be investigated following a genuine employee complaint or an incident referred to the HSE. Businesses in the 'higher-risk' categories (e.g. construction and agriculture) or those who have a track record of poor performance, will be subject to 'proactive' inspections.

RELATIONSHIP BETWEEN ENGLISH LAW AND EUROPEAN UNION LAW

Most of the laws that are included in this textbook refer to the law of England and Wales. However, the EU is a body that has established many legislative initiatives leading to changes to domestic law or requiring domestic law to incorporate new legislation. Much of the law relating to discrimination, working time, consultation requirements, and the transfer of undertakings has been inspired by EU law as its source. Therefore, to be an employment lawyer or a person heavily involved in employment law issues, also requires that individual to have a good knowledge of EU law and the judgments of the Court of Justice of the European Union.

On-the-spot question

 Consider how interlinked domestic employment law is with EU parent laws. What are the potential barriers created by these dual sources of law?

CONCLUSION

This chapter has identified several important institutions that are involved in resolving employment disputes. This book continues by identifying the nature and content of employment contracts, and how to find the various sources that affect both parties' rights and obligations at work.

FURTHER READING

Boon, A., Urwin, P. and Karuk, V. (2011) 'What Difference Does it Make? Facilitative Judicial Mediation of Discrimination Cases in Employment Tribunals', *Industrial Law Journal*, Vol. 40, p. 45.
The article critiques judicial mechanisms to resolve disputes through mediation with ACAS conciliation techniques.

Latreille, P., Latreille, J. and Knight, K. (2005) 'Making a Difference? Legal Representation in Employment Tribunals Cases: Evidence from a Survey of Representatives', *Industrial Law Journal*, Vol. 30, p. 308.
The article considers the impact on a case of the choice of representative in tribunal action.

Central Arbitration Committee (www.cac.gov.uk/)

Employment Tribunals (www.employmenttribunals.gov.uk/)

Employment Appeal Tribunal (www.employmentappeals.gov.uk/)

Equality and Human Rights Commission (www.equalityhumanrights.com)

Health and Safety Executive (www.hse.gov.uk/)

Chapter 3
Contracts of employment: terms and sources

LEARNING OUTCOMES

Having read this chapter you should be in a position to:

- identify the main sources of terms and conditions of the contract of employment;
- explain the methods used by the courts to imply terms into a contract;
- differentiate between obligations and rights, implied in the contract of employment, and imposed on employers and employees;
- identify which elements of a collective bargaining agreement may be enforced by an employee as part of the individual contract of employment.

MIND MAP

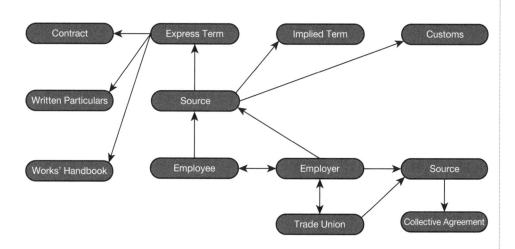

INTRODUCTION

This chapter begins the process of identifying the contents of the contract of employment, the various sources which establish the rights and responsibilities imposed on the parties, and the significance of implied terms which can substantially affect the contract. The most obvious source of employment terms are those contained in the written contract and those identified in the written statement of particulars as required in ERA 1996 s.1. Of course, it would be impractical to attempt to include all contractual terms and conditions in one written document, and therefore implied terms, customs and conventions may each provide obligations on the employer and employee.

Key Definition: Implied terms

It would be practically impossible to include every term in a written or expressed contract. Therefore, implied terms that are fundamental/obvious aspects of the employment relationship are included in the contract. Implied terms impose rights and obligations on the employer and employee.

Contracts of employment are based on classic contractual principles such as freedom of contract, and indeed, the parties are free to identify the terms by which they are willing to be bound, and no one can be forced to agree to a contract to which he or she does not agree. However, it is always worth recognising the imbalance of the power relationship between the parties, and it would generally be the employer who decides on which terms the relationship will be based. The individual, save for relatively few powerful workers, will largely be in a 'take it or leave it' situation.

SOURCES OF TERMS

You must appreciate the sources of the contract of employment and their contents because many employment disputes will require reference to the agreement that has been made between the parties. The most obvious source would be the actual contract of employment provided to the individual by the employer. Within eight weeks of beginning employment, an employee is entitled to a 'written statement of particulars' as provided for in ERA 1996 s.1. There are also other written sources that may be used including **collective agreements** established between the employer and, for example, a recognised trade union. Terms and conditions of employment may be incorporated through an organisational intranet/works' handbook. Further, it is especially important to recognise the role of implied terms in employment relationships. Judicial action, particularly in the 1970s and 80s, led to the creation/identification of many implied terms.

> **Key Definition: Collective agreement**
>
> An employer and a trade union may agree to negotiate on terms and conditions at work, which may apply just to the members of the union or may apply to all workers. Collective agreements, and their details, are usually identified in the contract of employment.

Awareness of the sources of terms will assist you significantly when you are dealing with workplace disputes and/or answering employment assessments in higher education courses.

Express terms

By their very nature **express terms** are expressed somewhere between the parties. Such a term may have been identified in oral negotiations, most likely it will have been included in the contract of employment, statement of written particulars provided to the individual, or letter of engagement. But remember, with the exception of certain statutory implied terms which the parties cannot override, an express term will take precedence over an implied term. Terms expressed in the contract will likely include (among others) pay, hours and place of work, line management and employee responsibilities, grievance procedures, any **restraint of trade** provisions, and ownership of intellectual property produced at work.

> **Key Definition: Restraint of trade**
>
> A restraint of trade is an agreement where the individual will not compete against his or her employer for a specified period of time and within a specified geographical area/industry. This is usually incorporated through a contractual clause. To be enforceable, the clause must protect a 'proprietary interest' rather than general commercial 'know-how'.

> **Key Definition: Express terms**
>
> The most significant details of the employment contract – the hours worked, pay, holiday entitlement and so on are usually expressed in the contract. Terms may be expressed in writing or made verbally.

Statement of written particulars

The legislation governing many aspects of employment law (ERA 1996) requires that an employee whose employment continues for a month or more must be provided (within eight weeks of the employment beginning) with a statement of written particulars – these are key aspects of the employment relationship. Section 1 is a statement of initial employment particulars and below is the list. It comes from an abridged version of section 1 of the Employment Rights Act 1996.

(3) The statement shall contain particulars of—
  (a) the names of the employer and employee,
  (b) the date when the employment began, and
  (c) the date on which the employee's period of continuous employment began (taking into account any employment with a previous employer which counts towards that period).

(4) The statement shall also contain particulars, as at a specified date not more than seven days before the statement (or the instalment containing them) is given, of –
  (a) the scale or rate of remuneration or the method of calculating remuneration,
  (b) the intervals at which remuneration is paid (that is, weekly, monthly or other specified intervals),
  (c) any terms and conditions relating to hours of work (including any terms and conditions relating to normal working hours),
  (d) any terms and conditions relating to any of the following—
    (i)   entitlement to holidays, including public holidays, and holiday pay (the particulars given being sufficient to enable the employee's entitlement, including any entitlement to accrued holiday pay on the termination of employment, to be precisely calculated),
    (ii)   incapacity for work due to sickness or injury, including any provision for sick pay, and
    (iii) pensions and pension schemes,
  (e) the length of notice which the employee is obliged to give and entitled to receive to terminate his contract of employment,
  (f)   the title of the job which the employee is employed to do or a brief description of the work for which he is employed,
  (g) where the employment is not intended to be permanent, the period for which it is expected to continue or, if it is for a fixed term, the date when it is to end,
  (h) either the place of work or, where the employee is required or permitted to work at various places, an indication of that and of the address of the employer,
  (j)   any collective agreements which directly affect the terms and conditions of the employment including, where the employer is not a party, the persons by whom they were made.

On-the-spot question

 How many individuals receive neither a written contract nor statement of written particulars and what are the potential consequences for their rights and responsibilities?

Works' handbook

A works' handbook is a convenient mechanism in which employers can place information regarding employment policies and procedures, and which is accessible to individuals, often through a staff intranet. It will identify which elements may be subject to changes, and such (non-contractual) changes in this document can be identified to individuals more conveniently than trying to amend written contracts.

Works' handbooks may also identify collective agreements between an employer and a bargaining unit (such as a trades union). However, the content and enforceability of works' handbooks compared with collective bargaining agreements differ on the basis that a works' handbook is unilaterally established by the employer.

Collective agreements

Unlike individually negotiated terms between the employer and individual, a collective agreement is an agreement made between the employer and an employees' representative body (usually a trades union) regarding terms and conditions at work (via collective bargaining – see Figure 3.1). Agreements made this way may simplify negotiations between the employer and workforce as agreements are made between two parties rather than the employer with each individual worker. Further, these agreements can extend beyond the members of the relevant trade union to non-members in what is called a 'bargaining unit'. Some terms and conditions may be incorporated into individual contracts of employment and others may not. Where the parties wish for the terms to be incorporated into individual contracts of employment, they can be referred to in the written statement of particulars. Most collective agreements are binding 'in honour only' and as such, they are not enforceable by the individual, although they must be reasonably accessible to employees (ERA 1996 s. 6).

Generally, procedural agreements regulate the relationship between the bargaining unit and the employer, deal with issues relating to resolving disputes, the status of trades unions, etc. Substantive agreements, on the other hand, deal with issues such as wages, conditions of work, holiday entitlement etc. Note however, it may not always be readily evident which is a procedural and which is a substantive agreement.

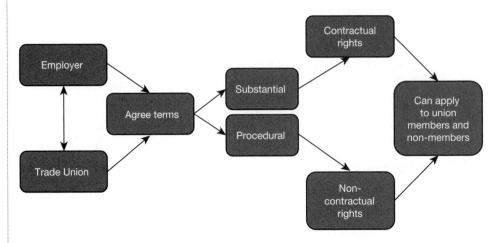

Figure 3.1 Collective bargaining relationships

KEY CASE ANALYSIS: *Allen v TRW Systems* [2013]
UKEAT/0083/12

Background

- TRW agreed a policy in 1999 with its work council regarding enhanced redundancy (severance) payments.
- The policy was included in the employee works handbook and identified in correspondence between the employer and workforce.
- The employees argued that these measures meant the payments were part of their contractual rights and the employer argued that they were not so incorporated as they had not been referred to in the employees written statement of terms.

Principle established

- The Employment Appeal Tribunal (EAT) held the terms were incorporated into the employees' contracts.
- The employer's actions were consistent with a course of action that would have provided the employees with a reasonable expectation that payments would be made with regard to the works' handbook.

The EAT followed *Keeley v Fosroc International* [2006] EWCA Civ. 1277, where the Court of Appeal held that there was nothing in principle preventing severance payments being incorporated through a works' handbook rather than a statement of contract terms.

Changes to the contract

Unilateral changes by the employer to the contract of employment are not permitted. However, where the employee has consented to changes in relation to the details of the written statement of particulars, the employer is required to provide written notification to the affected employee within one month of the change (ERA 1996 s. 4).

Where an employer has failed to provide the written statement of particulars, or where an incomplete statement is issued, ERA 1996 s. 11 requires the tribunal to determine the missing or incomplete particulars. Further, in such a situation where the employer has failed in their duty to provide the particulars, in any subsequent proceedings under Employment Act 2002 Sch. 5, the tribunal is obliged to provide or to increase an award of between two weeks' pay and four weeks' pay (where just and equitable to do so).

Customs/practices

Customs are not a particularly common way of incorporating terms into a contract of employment, but may be used where practices are common in either an employer's particular business, or in an industry. They are usually not agreed in any overt way, but over a period of time have become accustomed practice. An employer, for example, may have no formal agreement to provide employees with a reference when they leave the employment, but over time this has become an accepted course of conduct. In *Solihull Metropolitan Borough Council v National Union of Teachers* [1985] IRLR 211, the trade union instructed its members not to take part in certain voluntary activities including attending meetings outside of the teachers' regular hours of work. In an action by the Council against the trade union for inducing the teachers to breach their contract, when considering a defence that these voluntary actions were not part of the contract, the court held that the duties undertaken were part of the contract. They had been undertaken for such a long time that they had been incorporated into the teachers' contracts.

IMPLIED TERMS

As noted above, the written particulars, and even a written contract of employment, will not contain all the terms by which the parties are bound. There have been many implied terms in contracts of employment through works' handbooks, custom, statute and the courts.

Statutorily implied terms are imposed by parliament and employers may not override these through an express term (the courts imply the term through law). An example of a term implied through statute is s.66 of EA 2010 which imposes a sex equality clause into the contracts of men and women at work.

There are two main ways in which the courts will imply terms.

1   The first reason is business efficacy. The term being implied is necessary to make the contract work and while established in *The Moorcock* [1889] 14 PD 64, it is demonstrated in employment relationships in the implied term of mutual trust and confidence.
2   The second reason is because the term to be implied is so obvious it need not be expressed or it 'goes without saying'. This was established as a contractual principle in *Shirlaw v Southern Foundries* [1939] 2 KB 206 but can be seen in employment relationships with regards to provision for sick pay. The contract may be silent on the duration of payment of sick pay, but it will be implied that this will be applicable for a reasonable time and not paid forever. These examples are where the courts imply terms through the facts of the case.

Some of the most significant implied terms are listed here (but this is certainly not an exhaustive list).

Implied terms on employees

- Maintain mutual trust and confidence (*Coombes v Isle of Wight Tourist Board* [1976] IRLR 413).
- Duty to obey a lawful and reasonable order (*Macari v Celtic Football and Athletic Co. Ltd.* [1999] ScotCS 138).
- Duty of cooperation and adapting to new working conditions/techniques (*Cresswell v Board of Inland Revenue* [1984] IRLR 190).
- Fidelity (*Boston Deep Sea Fishing and Ice Co. v Ansell* (1888) 39 Ch. D 339).

Maintain mutual trust and confidence

Trust and confidence is one of the most significant implied terms, and as the name suggests, is applicable to both the employer and employee. In *Woods v WM Car Services* [1981] ICR 666 EAT, it was held that 'employers will not, without reasonable and proper cause, conduct themselves in a manner calculated or likely to destroy or seriously damage the relationship of confidence and trust between employer and employee' (per Browne-Wilkinson J p. 670).

This is one of the most significant implied terms as it underpins the employment relationship. However, the Court of Appeal in *Leach v OFCOM* [2012] EWCA Civ. 959 stated that the mere breakdown of trust between the parties will not always be held as a substantial and/or sufficient reason to justify a dismissal.

There are many examples of this implied term in an employment relationship. Typically, employers trust their employees with money, access to customers, access to suppliers, and access to confidential information. Employers must be able to trust their employees not to abuse their position of authority, and that employees will conduct themselves in a manner which is respectful of their employer. This is particularly relevant in the modern age with the use of social media and disclosure of information regarding employment. Trust and confidence ensures that the employer treats employees with respect, and prevents activities such as verbal and physical abuse, harassment, and bullying. Employers may also be in breach of this implied term where they fail to provide a grievance procedure whereby employees may complain about activities at work and reasonably expect that it is dealt with in a fair and transparent manner (see *Goold Ltd v McConnell* [1995] IRLR 516).

Duty to obey

Employees are under a duty to obey the lawful and reasonable instructions of the employer. Lawful instructions are usually those that an employer could expect the employee to undertake when requested. In *Morrish v Henleys (Folkstone) Ltd* [1973] 2 All ER 127, it was not lawful for an employer to sanction an employee who refused to falsify company records to 'assist' the employer. A reasonable instruction would generally be one which relates to an express term of the contract and, again, one which the employee would be expected to undertake as part of his/ her duties.

Cooperation with the employer

The employment relationship is dynamic, and due to its changing nature, the responsibilities of the parties may change over time. It is also, as demonstrated in this chapter, a realistic and practical necessity, that express terms in a contract will not cover each and every element. The parties must cooperate with each other to ensure that the relationship continues successfully. Therefore, employees must obey the lawful and reasonable instructions of their employer, but they must also cooperate with them. Cooperation could involve a request by an employer to undertake overtime work (for example in an emergency where a particular contract must be fulfilled immediately). It may also involve an employee changing to new working conditions or new ways of working. While new ways of working will often give some concern to employees, especially when this necessitates learning new skills such as the use of technology, the employer may require the employee to develop their skills as part of this requirement of cooperation; indeed, it is essential that employers can adapt their business to react to changes in working practices, but the employer is also under a corresponding duty to provide effective training to ensure the employees can adapt.

KEY CASE ANALYSIS: *Cresswell v Board of Inland Revenue* **[1984] IRLR 190**

Background

- Cresswell was employed by the Inland Revenue as a tax officer. His duties included using a paper-based filing system.
- As part of technological changes in working practices, the Inland Revenue introduced a computer based system for its PAYE system.
- Cresswell refused to operate the new system and claimed the contract merely required him to use the paper-based system.
- The Inland Revenue suspended Cresswell without pay until he was prepared to operate the new system.
- Cresswell brought a claim seeking a declaration that he was not bound to operate the new system, and that the Inland Revenue was in breach of its contract by suspending him without pay.

Principle established

It was held that an employer had a unilateral right to alter the contract in the interests of technological changes, insofar as training and time for adaptation is provided. Walton J remarked 'In an age when the computer has forced its way into the school room and where electronic games are played by school children in their own homes as a matter of everyday occurrence, it can hardly be considered that to ask an employee to acquire basic skills as to retrieving information from a computer or feeding such information into a computer is something in the slightest esoteric or, even nowadays, unusual' (p. 195).

Fidelity

Employees owe a duty of faithful service to their principal employer. This creates a system of loyalty where employees work for their employer, and any request to work for a competing employer must be accepted before such work may be undertaken. For example, a typical working week in the United Kingdom may involve 37–40 hours, over a five-day period. It is not impossible that some employees may wish to work longer hours to maximise their earning capacity. Where such hours are not readily available by the principal employer, an employee may seek to obtain work, using their skills and experience, working for a second employer. The implied duty of fidelity will prevent this, without an express agreement by the first/principal employer.

Key Definition: Fidelity

A term implied into contracts between an employer and employee where the employee will provide their service exclusively for this 'principal' employer. The employee may not, without the express permission of the employer, work in competition with the principal employer.

A practical reason behind this implied term is that an employer may require an employee to undertake overtime work, the employee may have access to confidential information, and an employee may have relations with the employer's clients and customers which may be compromised if they were to work for an alternative, competing, employer. The issue regarding confidential information is important as employers may wish to protect such 'trade secrets' and have the ability to do so through seeking the award of an injunction through the courts. Indeed, in *Hivac Ltd v Park Royal Scientific Instruments Ltd* [1946] 1 Ch. 169, even the near impossibility that commercial secrets could be disclosed to a competitor was still sufficient to lead to a breach of contract by the employees for undertaking the work.

The duty requires that information available to employees, such as the customer and client details of an employer may not be taken by an employee, particularly where this information is being removed in furtherance of establishing a competing business (see *Roger Bullivant Ltd v Ellis* [1987] ICR 464). Increasingly, employers are no longer simply relying on this implied term, but rather including express terms into a contract to ensure that employees do not work for competing employers during the course of their employment, and, as the implied term operates during the course of employment, to prevent this confidential information being used against the employer, a post-contractual 'restraint of trade' clause is frequently being incorporated into the contract to extend this protection after the employment relationship has been terminated.

On-the-spot question

 Being implied, do you think that many individuals would appreciate the extent of these terms and further, given their significance, would it not be appropriate for these to be expressly stated in the contract?

RESTRAINT OF TRADE CLAUSES

The employee's duty of fidelity provides that he/she will not unfairly compete with the employer or work directly in competition while employed. Problems arise when the employees' activities take place in their own time, not simply during employment. The following two cases provide a comparison in approaches to breach of this duty:

1   Hivac v Park Royal Scientific Instruments [1946] Ch. 169: five employees of Hivac sought to work on Sundays, their day off from employment, with Park who was the sole competitor of Hivac. These were skilled employees whose expertise was used by their employer's competitor. Hivac sought an injunction to prevent the five employees from working for Park on the basis that such an engagement breached the implied term of fidelity. It was held in the Court of Appeal that the employees had duties of good faith and fidelity, and these were breached by working for their employer's competitor, even though the work took place on their day of rest.

2   Nova Plastics Limited v Froggatt [1982] IRLR 146: demonstrated that where an employee was dismissed following the employer's discovery that the employee was working for a competitor in his own time, the employee's action must have caused the employer's business 'substantial harm' in order to breach the duty of fidelity. In this case, the Court of Appeal held the employee's actions had not caused this level of harm.

A restraint of trade clause is a post-contractual clause in which the employee is restricted from competing with the employer – either from setting up a business or working for a competitor – for a set period of time and in a limited geographical area. Due to such clauses being contrary to public policy, the length of time and geographical area are inversely proportional. This means the longer the period of time for which the restraint of trade clause applies, the smaller the geographical area. The broader the geographical area that the clause covers, the shorter the period of time for its application. Further, the clause will only be applied for as long as is necessary to protect the employer's legitimate interests. The courts will not allow an unfair or unreasonable restraint of trade clause to be applied.

To enable a restraint of trade clause to be effective, the employer must only seek to protect a 'proprietary interest'. This means that some specific confidential information or trade secret can be protected, but not a general skill and the know-how that the employee will have gained during the course of employment. It is also worth remembering the case of *RS Components v Irwin* [1974] 1 All ER 41, where an employer was able to force employees to agree to a new contract incorporating a restraint of trade clause, in order to protect its proprietary interests. Those employees who refused to sign, including Irwin, were fairly dismissed for 'some of other substantial reason' under ERA 1996 s. 98.

> **Key Definition: Garden leave**
>
> A garden leave arrangement is where an employer can ensure, with greater certainty than through a restraint of trade clause (which may be rejected by the courts), an employee does not work in competition with them. It is essentially an extended period of notice where the employee is not provided with any further work, but they are paid their salary to stay in their garden.

Where an employer may fear that a restraint of trade clause may not be effective, or could be open to question by a court, they may decide to use a **garden leave** clause. This is effective in that the individual is paid his/her salary and has full contractual benefits while on the leave, but the individual does not work and may not work for a competitor or go into business on their own account during that period. Ostensibly, the individual is paid to stay at home (and occupy him/herself in the garden). It may be more expensive (in relation to pay), but it guarantees protection for the employer as it is not subject to the 'proprietary interest' requirement of a restraint of trade clause.

Implied terms on an employer

- Maintain mutual trust and confidence (*Malik v Bank of Credit and Commerce International* [1997] UKHL 23).
- Duty to maintain the health and safety of workers.
- Duty to pay wages at a reasonable rate and within a reasonable time.
- Duty to pay a fair proportion of wages where an employee's industrial action is accepted by the employer (*Miles v Wakefield MDC* [1987] IRLR 193).
- Exceptionally (due to the nature of the employment) to provide work (*Clayton & Waller v Oliver* [1930] AC 209).

Maintain mutual trust and confidence

This has already been identified above, but the *Malik* case is important as it furthers the requirement of trust and confidence to the directors of the company not to operate that company in a wrongful and fraudulent manner. Malik was a former employee of the disgraced bank and suffered financial hardship in obtaining alternative employment after the collapse of the bank due to the 'stigma' of his association with his former employers. It is important to recognise that the House of Lords, when making this judgment, identified that this case was held specifically on its facts and did not establish a general principle of law. However, the case is effective in demonstrating the extent to which an employer must maintain the trust and confidence of its employees.

Maintain the health and safety of workers

The statutory Health and Safety at Work etc. Act 1974 (among others) and the common law tort of negligence each provide obligations on an employer to protect the health and safety of employees (and this extends to non-employees too). The duties on employers may be included as part of the contract (e.g. ERA 1996 s. 100, which renders dismissal of an employee for leaving work because of a reasonable belief that they may be in serious and imminent danger automatically unfair), but most of the cases involving the employer's negligence are derived from torts. Simply remember at this stage, contract law can provide damages for financial losses arising from injury. It may well be that in an industrial injury, the employee suffers pain and distress, perhaps even losing a limb, an eye, or receiving a fatal injury. In such instances, the damages available in contract are limited. Damages in torts can cover pain and suffering and other losses, and are not limited to financial loss. Therefore, many claimants will seek damages in torts rather than contract, for a breach of health and safety which has caused them injury and loss.

The health and safety requirements imposed on employers ensure that the employer provides a safe system of work and effective supervision, that the employee and their colleagues are competent, and that adequate safety equipment and protective devices are provided to reduce the possibility of injury. As with any claim of negligence, the threefold test is applied, as is the test of whether the employer is vicariously liable for the torts of their employees, and the employer, as defendant, has the ability to defend themselves through consent and contributory negligence of the claimant employee. This is further relevant when considering the distinction between contractual and tortious liability. An employer may be in breach of the contract to protect the health and safety of individuals, even where the individual has not suffered injury or loss. The individual would have a right to claim a remedy if they were dismissed on the basis of not following the employer's order, which may have compromised his/her health and safety. To hold an employer liable in torts, and to successfully recover a damages payment, the individual must have suffered loss or injury.

Pay wages

The contract of employment will identify clearly the payment of wages, their frequency, and an itemised pay statement identifying any required deductions such as income tax, National Insurance, and pension contributions (required by ERA 1996 s. 8). As wages are such a fundamental part of the employment relationship they are most likely to be identified in an expressed rather than implied term. However, issues such as payment for overtime work, payments for accrued holiday pay (owed on the termination of the contract), and expenses incurred when carrying out the employer's lawful instructions, may form the basis of implied terms.

Provide work

There is generally no obligation on an employer to provide work. In so far as the employer provides the individual with his/her wages, the employer has satisfied the requirements of the contract. A quote that is often provided to establish this point, is that of Asquith J in *Collier v Sunday Referee Publishing Co Ltd* [1940] 2 KB 647: 'Provided I pay my cook her wages regularly, she cannot complain if I choose to take any or all of my meals out.'

The exception to this general rule is where the employee is paid commissions, received as part of their work. For example, an estate agent who is in the business of selling property, may receive commissions on the basis of the value of the properties sold. This is part of his/her income, and it is quite possible that he/she is paid a relatively low 'basic' wage, which is then supplemented through these commissions. If the employer does not allow the employee to work, the agent would be unable to earn the commissions, and therefore it would be implied in the contract that the employer would provide this employee with work. Another example is an individual employed in the entertainment industry who requires work to maintain their public profile. Finally (although this is by no means an exhaustive list) medical professionals will have to be provided with work to maintain their skills and knowledge of, for example, new medical procedures.

FIXED-TERM CONTRACTS

The Fixed-term Employees (Prevention of Less Favourable Treatment) Regulations 2002 provide that where an individual is engaged under a succession of fixed-term contracts, the contract will become permanent after four years of continuous service. An employer may disagree with the permanency of the contract where such engagement on a fixed-term basis is 'objectively justified'. However, where the employee is engaged on a training scheme arranged by the government or is funded by the European Community, periods of works do not count in the calculation of this four-year period of employment (see *Hudson v Department of Work and Pensions* [2012] EWCA Civ. 1416).

CONCLUSION

The sources of the terms and conditions underpinning the employment relationship are naturally of great importance in regulating the responsibility of each party. They identify express terms (those which are among the most significant) and also implied terms (used to give further detail to the relationship and may be implied as they 'go without saying'). The sources of terms and conditions of work further include collective bargaining agreements and these will be particularly important in Chapter 10 when we consider industrial action.

Having identified the sources of terms, the book now continues by looking at another fundamental aspect of employment law – the employment status of individuals. Many protective rights, such as unfair dismissal and redundancy, along with the implied terms identified in this chapter, may only be available to those individuals with the employment status of 'employee'. It is therefore essential that you understand how the law differentiates between 'employees', 'workers' and 'independent contractors'.

FURTHER READING

Jefferson, M. (1997) 'Restraint of Trade: Dismissal and Drafting', *Industrial Law Journal*, Vol. 26, No.1, p. 62.
A paper reviewing case authority on the application of restraint of trade clauses in instances of wrongful dismissal.

Lindsay, Hon. Justice. (2001) 'The Implied Term of Trust and Confidence', *Industrial Law Journal*, Vol. 30, No.1, p. 1.
An article written by the (then) President of the EAT critiquing the judicial development of the implied term of trust and confidence.

Chapter 4
Employment status

LEARNING OBJECTIVES

After reading this chapter you should be able to:

- explain the sources used to determine the employment status of an individual;
- identify reasons for the importance of the distinction between employee; independent contractor and worker status;
- explain the evolution of the 'control' test to the 'right to control' test;
- apply the three tests established in the *Ready Mixed Concrete* case;
- identify the case *Montgomery v Johnson Underwood* as the leading case establishing two very important, preliminary tests for employee status – (1) the existence of control; and (2) mutuality of obligations between the parties.

MIND MAP

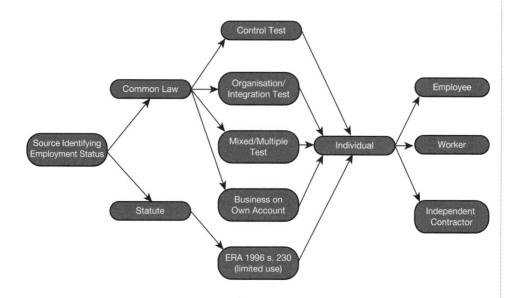

INTRODUCTION

There are many employment rights that are available to individuals working in Great Britain. Some are so important that they are available to all individuals personally engaged to perform work, e.g. health and safety rights, certain equality rights, etc. However, many of the most significant are only available to individuals with '**employee**' employment status.

Key Definition: Employee

An individual who is engaged by an employer under a 'contract of service.' They have access to a greater number of rights than an independent contractor, but are also subject to a greater range of implied terms in the contract.

Where both the employer and the individual agree with the employment status, there is no need for further debate. However, many individuals may not necessarily know of their employment status, and many more may not understand how employment status affects their rights at work. Therefore, this is a crucial subject for identifying many employment rights and obligations, but see the judgment from Denning LJ below and you will begin to understand the complexity and problems it brings:

> It is often easy to recognise a contract of service (employee) when you see it, but difficult to say wherein the difference lies. A ship's master, a chauffer, and a reporter on the staff of a newspaper are all employed under a contract of service; but a ship's pilot, a taximan, and a newspaper contributor are employed under a contract for services.
>
> Lord Denning – Stevenson, Jordan and Harrison Ltd v
> Macdonald and Evans [1952] 1 TLR 101

On-the-spot question

 Given its importance, why do think the tribunals have been given so much discretion in deciding the employment status of an individual?

EMPLOYMENT STATUS

One of the most important aspects of employment relations is the status of the individual engaged by the employer. In English law, such an individual may be labelled as:

- an employee;
- an **independent contractor**; or
- a worker.

These 'labels' affect the individual and employer in numerous ways. For example, an employee has access to statutory protections regarding unfair dismissal, redundancy, maternity pay, but they are also subject to various implied terms in the contract that may have significant implications for their duties and employment relationship.

Key Definition: Independent contractor

An individual who is in business of their own account and is engaged by an employer under a 'contract for services'. The independent contractor is genuinely self-employed and consequently has access to fewer protective employment rights. However, they benefit from more favourable tax regulations and may work for several employers – maximising their income stream.

An employer may be held vicariously liable for torts committed by an employee, they are subject to a higher standard of care for the protection of an employee's health and safety at work, they are subject also to the implied term of trust and confidence, and an employer is responsible for the deduction of tax and National Insurance payments for each employee.

Given the power held by an employer to provide the contract (and incorporate contractual terms and 'labels' of employment status), the use of labels identifying an individual as an 'employee' or an 'independent contractor' is indicative not conclusive. This prevents employers from evading legal liabilities by obtaining the acceptance of the label by an individual who may be unaware as to its legal implications and significance. In the case *Young & Woods v West* [1980] it was identified that the basic position adopted by the courts is that ' accepting . . . the label . . . (is) a guide and no more.' In *Ferguson v John Dawson & Partners (Contractors) Ltd* [1976] it was held that the label of 'independent contractor' should 'be disregarded entirely if the remainder of the contract terms point to the opposite conclusion'.

KEY CASE ANALYSIS: *Autoclenz Ltd v Belcher and Others* **[2011] UKSC 41**

Background

- Autoclenz ran a business cleaning cars for a company in the auction business.
- It engaged valeters to undertake this work, including Mr Belcher.
- The valeters signed a contract describing them as self-employed, it identified that Autoclenz had no obligation to offer future work, and the valeters were required to personally provide all the necessary cleaning equipment.
- The valeters were paid for each car cleaned, and they were responsible for payment of their own tax and National Insurance contributions.
- The employment status of the valeters had to be determined following a claim for holiday pay and payment at the national minimum wage rate.

Principle established

- The Supreme Court held that the valeters were engaged under a contract of employment.
- The reasoning of the judgment was that, despite the terms of the contract to the contrary (that the individuals were self-employed, the employer had no **mutuality of) obligation** to provide further work, etc.), contracts of employment were specific and were not to be treated in the same way as commercial contracts. This was because of inequality of bargaining power between the parties.
- The courts should search for the 'true intention of the parties'.
- Accordingly, the valeters, as employees, were entitled to the pay and at the appropriate level.

HOW TO IDENTIFY AN EMPLOYEE

It is not always easy to identify an employee. You may have thought that, given the significance that it plays in the access to fundamental rights and the obligations it may impose on the parties, clear guidance would be available. However, we have to look to various sources – the contract of employment (which may or may not be available); statute (ERA 1996) and the common law. Also, reading through the various cases involving employment status may actually make you less certain about identifying an individual's employment status, as inconsistent decisions are common in tribunal awards. However, there have been tests developed by the courts that help answer the question and it is essential to be familiar with these as they will at least act as a guide (not definitive proof) as to how a tribunal is likely to determine employment status.

Contract of employment

Within eight weeks of starting work, an individual should be provided with written particulars of employment (ERA 1996 s. 1). This outlines various aspects of the working relationship such as:

(3) (a) the names of the employer and employee;
    (b) the date when the employment began; and
    (c) the date on which the employee's period of continuous employment began.
(4) (a) the scale or rate of remuneration or the method of calculating remuneration;
    (c) any terms and conditions relating to hours of work;
    (d) any terms and conditions relating to any of the following—
        (i)   entitlement to holidays, including public holidays, and holiday pay;
        (ii) incapacity for work due to sickness or injury, including any provision for sick pay; and
        (iii) pensions and pension schemes.
    (e) the length of notice which the employee is obliged to give and entitled to receive to terminate his contract of employment;
    (g) where the employment is not intended to be permanent, the period for which it is expected to continue or, if it is for a fixed term, the date when it is to end;
    (h) either the place of work or, where the employee is required or permitted to work at various places, an indication of that and of the address of the employer;
    (j) any collective agreements which directly affect the terms and conditions of the employment including, where the employer is not a party, the persons by whom they were made.

Note that this document may contain similar points to the contract of employment, but due to the many implied terms in employment relationships, it is not the contract. This document may label the individual as an employee, independent contractor or worker, but this is not conclusive proof – it is of persuasive authority only. In cases of unfair dismissal, redundancy, or discrimination, where no written statement of particulars has been provided by the start of the proceedings, a minimum of two weeks' wages, and a maximum of four weeks' wages (as of 1 February 2013 – to a maximum of £450 per week) is awarded (Employment Act 2002 s. 38).

Where the individual and the employer disagree as to the employment status, the tribunal will have to look to the true working relationship of the parties (the fact) and application of the statute and common law tests (the law). Therefore, in employment law, determining the status of an individual is a mix of law and fact.

Statutory definition

As statute law is the highest form of law, naturally it is important to start here. ERA 1996 s. 230 defines each of the three types of employment status. An employee is 'an individual who has entered into or works under (or, where the employment has ceased, worked under) a contract of employment'. Further, contract of employment is defined in s. 230(2) as 'a contract of service or apprenticeship, whether express or implied, and (if it is express) whether oral or in writing'.

The result is a very broad, essentially unusable test. However, this was the intention of the legislators. Being broad, it requires reference to the common law tests and this allows the law to develop to reflect changes in employment practices more quickly than legislation could possibly achieve. Given the organisational and technological developments in working practices in, for example, the last 30 years, the common law is the best place to adapt tests to determine employment status.

The common law

For the past 150 years the common law has attempted to create a test to identify the employment status of individuals. Griffiths LJ commented in *Lee Ting Sang v Chung Chi-Keung* [1990] IRLR 236 that determining employment status: 'has proved to be a most elusive question and despite a plethora of authorities the courts have not been able to devise a single test that will conclusively point to the distinction in all cases'.

Before we begin, it is important to recognise that the tribunals have been instructed not to apply the tests in a mechanical fashion (see *Hall v Lorimer* [1993] EWCA Civ. 25). What this means in practice, is that the tribunals, while being bound by precedent established in the higher courts, are the institutions that hear all of the evidence and ask appropriate questions. Having heard the evidence, the tribunal is entitled to attach whatever weighting it feels appropriate to the evidence. For example, one tribunal could find that an individual paying her own tax and National Insurance contributions was very important and led to a finding of status as an independent contractor. Similarly, another tribunal could decide that such payments being made was not significant and other factors were more important when finding the claimant as an employee.

When the courts first began the task, it was in the days of masters and servants. A servant (who in modern times would be called an employee) was under the control of the master (the employer). This led to the **control test**.

The control test

The test was initially created to identify an individual as an employee or as self-employed (an independent contractor). The greater the level of control exercisable by the employer over the individual's activities at work, the more likely the individual would be held as an employee. A definition of control as provided for in *Ready Mixed Concrete (South East) Ltd v Minister of Pensions and National Insurance* [1968] 2 QB 497 was 'the power of deciding the thing to be done, the way in which it shall be done, the means to be employed in doing it ... the time and place it shall be done'. Further, McKenna J commented in *Stevenson, Jordan and Harriso*n [1952], that control should be 'ultimate authority over the [individual] in the performance of his work [by] the employer so that he was subject to the latter's order and directions'.

Key Definition: Control test

A fundamental test establishing an individual's employment status as an employee. As a minimum, individuals must be subject to the employer's control and there must be mutuality of obligations between the parties for status as an 'employee' to be established.

In the case *Yewens v Noakes* (1880) 6 QBD 530, Bramwell LJ stated that an employee is 'a person subject to the command of his master (employer) as to the manner in which he shall do his work'. The test used today is the 'right to control'. It is important to recognise that individuals are considerably more skilled in the modern day than they were when the courts started to establish the common law tests for employment status. This evolution may be seen when considering the position of skilled workers, who may be hired to perform jobs that do not require an employer to control their actions. For example, surgeons, professional footballers, pilots, lawyers, etc. may be employees, yet it is unlikely that their employer will exercise (even if they could) that kind of control. Hence, the control test relates to the employer's ability to control when an individual works and which order tasks are completed, etc. rather than HOW to do the job.

It is also important to recognise that control does not necessarily mean 'direct supervision'. In the case of *Montgomery v Johnson Underwood Ltd* [2001] IRLR 269, control was deemed to be satisfied where work can be closely monitored by quantifying productivity. This is particularly important for those individuals who perhaps work outside of a regular office, and in the light of the influx of technological advancements that facilitate mobile working. Therefore direct 'day-to-day' control is not necessary (see *White & Todd v Troutbeck SA* [2013] UKEAT 0177/12).

KEY CASE ANALYSIS: *Walker v Crystal Palace Football Club* [1910]

Background

- Walker was a professional footballer contracted to Crystal Palace FC for a one-year agreement.
- Part of his contract required him to regularly attend training sessions and follow the rules of the club.
- During the contract Walker was injured and did not play again all season.
- Therefore, at the end of the one-year agreement, the contract was not extended or renewed.
- Walker wanted to claim compensation for his permanent incapacity but qualification for the benefit was restricted to individuals with employee status.
- Crystal Palace argued that Walker could not be an employee as they could exercise no control over a professional footballer.

Principle established

- The Court of Appeal held that Walker was an employee of the football club.
- The control test, as argued by the club, was an older, out-of-date way of using the test.
- The control test had evolved with skilled workers to the 'right to control' test. The club controlled Walker in when he trained, where he trained, if he played in a football match or was not selected, and Walker had to follow the rules of the club.
- Just because the employer could not force Walker to pass the ball or run in a given direction did not mean they did not control him.
- Skilled workers are engaged to provide their skill and as such they need less direct supervision than an unskilled worker.

On-the-spot question

? Imagine that a surgeon negligently removed the wrong fingers from a patient undergoing an operation. When the patient attempted to claim compensation due to the surgeon's negligence, would the surgeon be an employee (and so the patient can sue the hospital who employed them) or do you think a surgeon would be an independent contractor (and so any claim would have to be made against him/her personally)? How would you justify your answer?

In conclusion of this section, remember, the control test continues to be fundamental to establishing employment status, but it CANNOT be used in isolation. It is part of the wider 'mixed test' as outlined below.

On-the-spot question

 Do you feel confident in explaining how and why the 'control' test became the 'right to control' test?

The integration or organisation test

Given the advances in working practices, and the increase in skilled workers since the creation of the control test – meaning it could no longer be realistically used in isolation, judges tried to establish a modern test to determine employment status. Lord Denning attempted to clarify the situation in the case *Stevenson, Jordan and Harrison v Macdonald and Evans* [1952]. The case concerned the ownership of intellectual property rights – at a very basic level, intellectual property created at work by an employee belongs to the employer, if it is created by an independent contractor, it belongs to the contractor. In his judgment, Denning established that an employee is 'integrated' into an organisation, whereas an independent contractor operates on the periphery and is not 'part and parcel of the business'. However, Lord Denning did not define what he meant by the word 'integration' and this judgment led to even greater confusion rather than aiding clarity. As such, it is of very limited use in any practical sense – indeed McKenna J in *Ready Mixed Concrete* [1968] held that it 'raised more questions than it answered' – but it is important to be aware of its existence in the evolution of the common law tests.

While the integration test is of limited practical use (because of the deficiencies as identified above), it has been referred to more broadly in academic commentary. Collins (1990) has argued that pension contributions, for example, provide a 'badge of membership' of employment status and that they amount to a form of 'organisational integration'. Therefore, while limited, it is possible to understand what Denning meant when he established the test.

The mixed test

The case *Ready Mixed Concrete v Minister of Pensions and National Insurance* [1968] is a very important case as it established three questions that, when answered, will assist in determining the individual's employment status.

KEY CASE ANALYSIS" *Ready Mixed Concrete v Minister of Pensions and National Insurance* **[1968]**

Background

1   Ready Mixed Concrete manufactured and delivered concrete.
2   It engaged individuals labelled 'owner-drivers' for the delivery part of the business.
3   The drivers had no set hours of work; no fixed meal breaks; they had to wear company uniforms; they were subject to the reasonable orders of the company's management; they were obliged to maintain the lorries and keep them painted in the company colours.
4   The drivers wanted to know who was responsible for tax payments. This led to the court case.

Principle established

Mackenna J identified three tests which, when answered, would establish the employment status of the individual.

The three tests that should be applied are:

1   The servant agrees that, in consideration of a wage or other remuneration, he will provide his own work and skill in the performance of some service for his master.
2   He agrees, expressly or impliedly, that in the performance of that service he will be subject to the other's control in a sufficient degree to make that other master.
3   The other provisions of the contract are consistent with its being a contract of service.

What do the tests mean?

- The first test refers to what is commonly referred to now as mutuality of obligations. It is a requirement that an employee undertakes to work personally and the employer agrees to provide pay or to provide work.
- The second test is merely the inclusion of the right to control test as identified above.
- The third test is, perhaps, the most interesting of the three tests. Here it is the employment relationship and the tasks undertaken by the individual that is assessed. For example, in the case of O'Kelly v Trusthouse Forte plc [1983]

Key Definition: Mutuality of obligations

An essential feature of 'employee' status. An employee has a continuing obligation to undertake work or be available for work for the employer; and the employer has a corresponding obligation to provide work or provide pay to the employee.

ICR 728 it was held that payment of annual leave was consistent with the existence of a contract of service. Further, in the case of Carmichael v National Power plc [1999] UKHL 47, sickness, holiday pay, and pension arrangements for regular staff would not apply to independent contractors, hence these features were inconsistent with the existence of a contract of service (see Table 4.1).

It is important to remember that certain features will not, of themselves, be indicative either way as a consistent or inconsistent feature of employment status. An employer will generally be responsible for the payment of an employee's tax and National Insurance (Davies v New England College of Arundel [1977] ICR 6). However, while this is generally true, the case of Massey v Crown Life Insurance [1978] 1 WLR 676 demonstrated that such payments might also conclude with the individual being held as an independent contractor. It was not decisive to this individual's employment status.

- In the application of these tests, there is no certainty as to any court or tribunal's decision, but with reference to previous case law it is possible to understand the courts reasoning and justification for determining consistency and inconsistencies of a contract of service.

Table 4.1 Examples of consistent/inconsistent features of a contract of service

Consistent features	Inconsistent features
Tax and National Insurance contributions deducted at source (PAYE)	Pricing each job individually
Able to claim expenses	Ability to provide a substitute/ Sub-contract the work
Wearing company uniform	Investment in the business/ability to benefit from sound management
Subject to employer's disciplinary procedures	Obligation to provide own tools/materials
Obligation to follow the reasonable orders of the employer	No set hours of work
Payment of sickness, holiday pay, and pension arrangements	Ability to work concurrently for more than one employer without permission

Mutuality of obligations

A key element in establishing an individual as an employee is the mutuality of obligations between that person and the employer. *Montgomery v Johnson Underwood* [2001] defined mutuality of obligations as 'an irreducible minimum of mutual obligation in respect of the work in question'. Such mutual obligation involves 'each party to make promises . . . to the taking on of obligations, (thereby) creating adequate consideration for a contract of employment'. (Freedland, 2003).

To give an example, consider a typical employee working in an office with a requirement to be at their desk Monday–Friday, 9am–5.30pm. That employee has an obligation to be at work each weekday (or at least be available for work if the employer tells her to stay away from the office). The employer has a corresponding obligation to provide her with work (or pay as here there is no implied duty to provide her with work).

Now, consider the situation of an independent contractor. You have a problem with the sink in your house. You call a plumber who visits your house, fixes the problem, you pay him for completing the job, and he leaves. What would happen if the plumber visited your house the next day asking for the next job he is to complete? This would be a very peculiar situation. You had a problem with your sink, you contacted a professional tradesman (a plumber) to remedy the problem, and following completion of the task, the plumber left. There is no expectation of regular work or mutuality of obligations between you and the plumber. In *Nethermere v Gardiner Nethermere (St Neots) Ltd v Gardiner and Taverna* [1984] IRLR 240, it was held that 'any arrangement without any obligation for work to be done or provided could not be a contract of service'. Indeed, in that case Stephenson LJ commented that where work was consistently, and over a substantial period of time 'provided and accepted . . . it could infer a mutual obligation between the parties'.

This is the essence of the test – an employee has a reasonable expectation that they have to attend work and that work will be provided for them. An independent contractor has no such reasonable expectation; they are engaged to complete a specific service, they are paid gross (no deduction of tax is taken), and having completed the task with that employer they move on to the next job (and presumably a different employer). Working on a 'casual/as required' basis has usually led to the courts/tribunals holding that there is no mutuality between the parties – (*O'Kelly v Trusthouse Forte plc* [1983] and *Carmichael v National Power plc* [1999] are the case law authorities here).

Further, despite the use of precise language, there have been varying interpretations of the concept of mutuality of obligations. Two cases that are often contrasted are *Nethermere v Gardiner* [1984] and *O'Kelly v Trusthouse Forte* [1983]. In *Nethermere*, a broad interpretation of mutuality was adopted, emphasising as it did the legal impact of economic and psychological pressures on individuals. While in *O'Kelly*, a much more strict and narrow approach was used (see Leighton, 1984). This led to Freedland commenting that without the use of an intrinsic approach to discovering the existence of mutuality of obligations, it will continue to be 'as elusive as the search for the philosopher's stone' (see Freedland, 2003).

Business on own account

The courts also considered that some individuals who were working and doing the same job as employees had been registered (or at times re-registered) as independent contractors. As noted above, there are tax and work advantages for some individuals (and their employers) to work as an independent contractor rather than an employee. However, a key determining factor between employees and independent contractors is that employees are not in business on their own account. They most likely have no investment in the business, are not exposed to financial risk, do not have to provide their own tools in completion of tasks at work, and have no opportunity for profiting from sound management, and they are not allowed to sub-contract – contracts of employment are contracts of personal service. Indeed, Cooke J in *Market Investigations Ltd v Minister of Social Security* [1969] 2 QB 173 stated:

> The fundamental test to be applied is this: 'Is the person who has engaged himself to perform these services performing them as a person in business on his own account?' If the answer to that question is 'yes', then the contract is a contract for services (independent contractor). If the answer is 'no', then the contract is a contract of service (employee).

In *Lee Ting Sang v Chung Chi-Keung* [1990], being in business on your own account included features such as the individual providing their own tools and equipment, pricing each job individually, engagement of assistants/helpers, and maintaining responsibility in, or the management of, the workplace. This includes the ability to benefit from sound management and may also incorporate an element of financial risk (see in *Stringfellow Restaurants Ltd v Quashie* [2012] EWCA Civ. 1735 regarding a lap-dancer who was paid directly by third parties (the customers) and therefore was not an employee due to the financial risk of being paid nothing).

PUTTING IT ALL TOGETHER

Given the above information, how do we identify with certainty the employment status of an individual? The short answer is, we don't! There is no one, irrefutable test that can be used. What we have to do is follow the tests that have been established and do our best in applying the principles identified (see Figure 4.1). Therefore, this is a sensible approach to follow:

- First, look at any contract/written particulars that is available, which labels the individual's employment status. Remember, however, that any label of employment status is indicative, NOT conclusive evidence.
- Then, review the actual working relationship of the parties using the available common law tests.
- The case *Montgomery v Johnson Underwood Ltd* [2001] is the leading authority on employment status. It provides that you must answer the following questions positively – (1) that there is an element of control exercisable by the employer (the right to control test); and (2) that there is mutuality of obligations between the parties.
- Having answered the *Montgomery* questions in the affirmative, apply the (last of the) three *Ready Mixed Concrete* [1968] questions. Examples of provisions of the contract which are consistent with it being a contract of employment include: where the individual is paid expenses, the existence

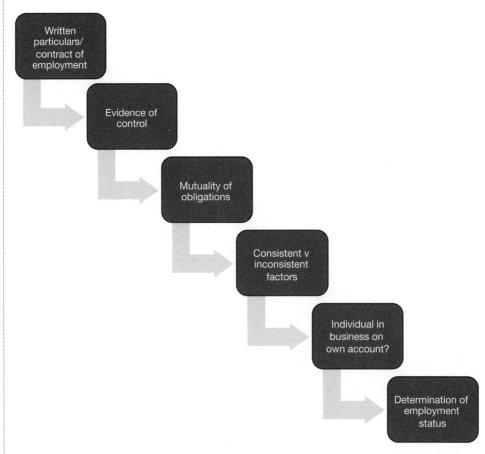

Figure 4.1 Flow chart – steps to discovering employment status

of a restraint of trade clause, where the individual has identifiable disciplinary procedures applied against them, etc.

- Remember – the tests are considered as a whole and what the tribunals/courts do is to 'paint an overall picture' of the employment relationship.

CONCLUSION

This chapter has identified the main features and determining factors to establish the employment status of an individual. Employment status is very important in employment law as it provides rights and obligations on both parties and therefore it often forms part of a discretely examinable topic. Ensure that you read as many case authorities as possible – this will give you examples of how cases have been decided and these will help you give as full an answer as possible.

FURTHER READING

Collins, H. (1990) 'Independent Contractors and the Challenge of Vertical Integration to Employment Protection Laws', *Oxford Journal Legal Studies*, Vol. 10, No. 3.
An article reviewing employment laws, developed around a paradigm of vertical integration in times of prosperity, and changes to this structure, and resultant problems, due to the economic downturn in the 1980s. It is an interesting study, particularly in relation to the current economic crisis.

Deakin, S. (2001) 'The Contract of Employment: A Study in Legal Evolution', *ESRC Centre for Business Research*, University of Cambridge, Working Paper No. 203.
Paper charting the development of employment status in relation to its common law history and statutory intervention.

Deakin, S. (2007) 'Does the "Personal Employment Contract" Provide a Basis for the Reunification of Employment Law?', *Industrial Law Journal*, Vol. 36, No. 1.
The article presents interesting ideas regarding a unified body of employment laws without the employment status distinction, focusing the argument on 'personal employment contracts'.

Freedland, M. R. (2003) *The Personal Employment Contract*, Oxford University Press.
A book reviewing the various forms of employment contracts, focusing in particular on the 'personal' dimension of such relationships.

Honeyball, S. (2011) *Employment Law Great Debates*, Palgrave Macmillan.
A detailed and analytical account of major employment issues. It is not an 'easy' book, however, it will give you a depth of analysis that textbooks cannot.

Chapter 5
Discrimination

LEARNING OBJECTIVES

After reading this chapter you should be able to:

- identify and explain the 'protected characteristics' and 'prohibited conduct' elements of EA 2010;
- explain the interaction between domestic law, law of the European Union, and laws derived from the UK's membership of the European Convention on Human Rights;
- identify the rights of individuals and specific remedies that may be sought for transgression of anti-discrimination legislation.

INTRODUCTION

The Equality Act (EA) 2010 protects people against discrimination (which is now considered to be a form of prohibitory conduct) on the basis of their protected characteristics (such as their sex, sexual orientation, race, religious or philosophical belief, and disability). The remit of EA 2010 is broader than simply employment relations, it also incorporates people's access to goods and services, but it is important to recognise that it applies before employment (at recruitment), during employment (e.g. the terms and conditions of employment/training/promotion), and when the employment relationship is to be terminated (selection for dismissal/subjecting the victim to a detriment).

Key Definition: Protected characteristics

The Equality Act 2010 established a range of actions that would be contrary to this piece of legislation. In order to qualify for this protection, the individual has to either possess the protected characteristic, be associated with a person in possession of the characteristic, or have been discriminated against because it was perceived that they possessed the characteristic.

MIND MAP

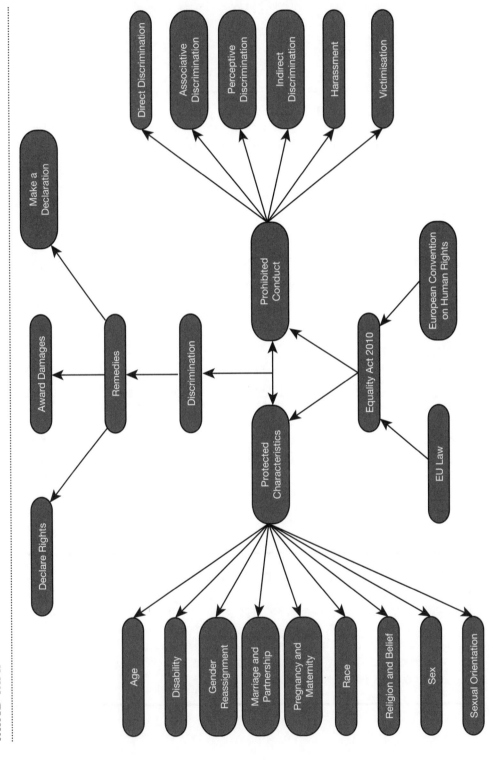

An example in practice: You are an employer and you wish to advertise to recruit a person to undertake a job in a call centre. You are aware that many of your customers complain when they cannot understand, or be understood, by the call operator. To prevent this occurrence, you advertise that a key requirement of the person taking on the job, is that their first language must be English (this will ensure proficiency in spoken and written English). The aim is to guarantee the person appointed can be understood and understand the callers.

In the above example, a discriminatory act has occurred through **direct discrimination**. When you advertised the vacancy, you stated that a criterion which had to be complied with in order to be considered for the job was that the person must have English as their first language. You simply meant that the call operator had to have a high level of proficiency in the English language. Communication was the key criteria here. However, what you have inadvertently done is to dissuade people whose first language was not English from applying. It is a very simple mistake, but one which will transgress EA 2010, possibly leading to a complaint to the Equality and Human Rights Commission, and also, will be very embarrassing for the business, which consequently may appear to operate a discriminatory recruitment policy.

Key Definition: Direct discrimination

This form of prohibited conduct exists where a person treats another less or unfavourably then they would have treated that person without the protected characteristic.

Discrimination therefore can occur deliberately – it could be through an innocent mistake, it can be disguised as a lawful activity – it may also be due to some prejudice against someone to whom the victim is associated with, or can be on the basis of some misguided assumption held by the perpetrator against the victim.

Discrimination laws are extremely important to the fair and lawful operation of businesses, and discriminatory activities by an employer can have negative effects for the business and far-reaching consequences for society. It is for these reasons, among many, many others, that employment lawyers need to have an awareness of anti-discrimination legislation, both domestically and those derived from the EU.

EQUALITY LAW

In October 2010 EA 2010 came into force. It repealed most of the previous anti-discrimination laws and attempted to standardise the forms of discriminatory behaviour, the tests to be applied to establish discrimination, and the groups of people (protected characteristics) who were protected. EA 2010 affects groups wider than just employees and employers, but as the focus of this chapter is on employment, the functioning of EA 2010 is limited to this group.

Protected characteristics

For an individual to be protected under EA 2010, he/she must possess (or in some cases be associated with a person with) a characteristic identified in the legislation. The specific characteristics protected are:

- Age (s. 5).
- Disability (s. 6): an individual possesses a disability that is a physical or mental impairment that has a substantial and long-term effect on their ability to carry out normal day-to-day activities. Employers are required to make 'reasonable adjustments' to accommodate individuals with a disability.
- Gender reassignment (s. 7): an individual who proposes to undergo, is currently undergoing, or who has undergone a process of reassigning their sex is protected against discrimination on the basis of this protected characteristic. Medical procedures are no longer necessary to qualify for protection – the individual must simply live permanently as the reassigned gender.
- Marriage and civil partnership (s. 8): single people are not protected.
- Pregnancy and maternity (ss. 72–76).
- Race (s. 9): this term includes 'colour; nationality; and ethnic or national origins'. The protected characteristic applies to a person of a particular racial group or persons of the same racial group.
- Religion or belief (s. 10): protection against discrimination is provided on the basis of an individual's choice of religion, religious beliefs (or non-belief), or other similar philosophical belief – be that a real or perceived belief.
- Sex (s. 11).
- Sexual orientation (s. 12): an individual's sexual orientation is their orientation towards persons of the same sex (homosexual), opposite sex (heterosexual), or both sexes (bisexual).

Prohibited conduct

Having established that the claimant possesses, is associated with a person who possesses, or where the defendant perceives that the claimant possesses a characteristic listed above, the defendant will breach the individual's rights where they commit or permit a form of **prohibited conduct** to take place.

Key Definition: Prohibited conduct

The codification of the anti-discrimination legislation through the Equality Act 2010 established a range of discriminatory activities as prohibited conduct – therefore they would be unlawful activities.

The types of behaviour that constitute prohibited conduct are:

Direct discrimination

This applies to all of the protected characteristics.

It occurs where a person (in this context, for example, the employer) treats another (for example, an employee) less favourably because of their protected characteristic than they would a person who does not possess the characteristic. Direct discrimination applies to actual, associated, or perceptive forms of less favourable treatment.

Generally, direct discrimination cannot be justified. However, exceptions do exist where discriminatory behaviour is necessary or a common sense approach is needed. The following examples apply.

1   The basis of an employee's age, where the behaviour is a proportionate means of achieving a legitimate aim.
2   Treating an individual with a disability more favourably than a person without the disability.
3   Direct discrimination may be justified due to the genuine **occupational requirements** of the job. For example, an otherwise act of direct sex discrimination may be explained as non-discriminatory where it is necessary to preserve privacy or decency (for example, a changing room attendant). An otherwise act of direct discrimination based on race may be explained as non-discriminatory where authenticity is required (for example in a Chinese/Indian/Mexican themed restaurant).

Key Definition: Occupational requirement

This is a defence to an otherwise discriminatory act, but the discrimination is justified as it is predicated on the nature of the employment, rather than (for example) the sex of the claimant and comparator.

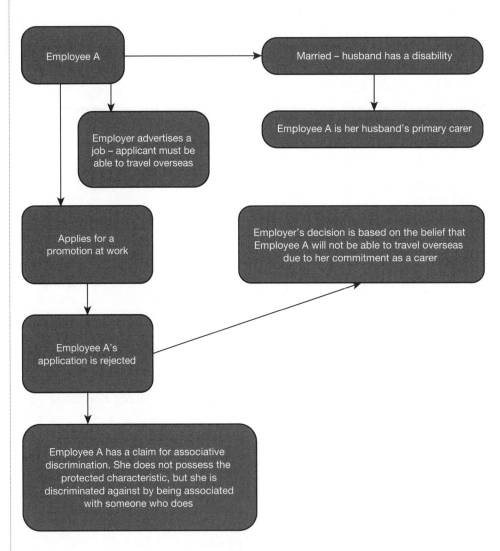

Figure 5.1 Example of associative discrimination

Associative discrimination

This applies to the protected characteristics, except marriage and civil partnership, and pregnancy and maternity. It allows an individual protection due to the characteristic of a person with whom they are associated. For example, it may be unlawful to discriminate against an employee because his wife has a disability and the employer believes the employee will have to take time away from work to provide her with care (see Figure 5.1).

Perceptive discrimination

Perceptive discrimination applies to the protected characteristics, except marriage and civil partnership, and pregnancy and maternity. It allows an individual protection against discrimination on the basis of a protected characteristic which they do not possess, but the person discriminating perceives that person to possess. For example, calling an individual at work a 'poof' (to refer to a person whose sexual orientation is homosexual) when in fact the individual subjected to the name-calling is heterosexual.

Indirect discrimination

This applies to the protected characteristics, except marriage and civil partnership, and pregnancy and maternity (although it may apply to the protected characteristic of indirect sex discrimination). It occurs where a seemingly neutral provision, criterion or practice is applied (to, for example, a job advertisement), which disadvantages people possessing a protected characteristic and cannot be objectively justified as a proportionate means of achieving a legitimate aim.

Key Definition: Indirect discrimination

This form of prohibited conduct exists where a seemingly neutral provision, criterion or practice is applied to everyone, but its effects disproportionately affect persons who share a protected characteristic. This puts them at a particular disadvantage, and the provision, criterion or practice is not a proportionate means of achieving a legitimate aim.

Harassment

Applies to the protected characteristics, except marriage and civil partnership, and pregnancy and maternity. The harassment may be sexual harassment, amount to less favourable treatment because of the sexual harassment or it may be related to sex or gender reassignment; or it may be related to a person's protected characteristic.

Harassment is unwanted conduct which is related to a protected characteristic and which has the purpose or effect of violating a person's dignity or creating an intimidating, hostile, degrading, humiliating or offensive environment (this is a subjective test). Importantly, the unwanted conduct does not have to be directed at the individual, nor does the individual have to personally possess the characteristic. Also, an act of a sufficiently serious nature may constitute harassment. Employers may find themselves vicariously liable for acts of harassment by their employees or agents where the employer was aware, or should have been aware, of the harassment and failed to take appropriate action (see Figure 5.2). A defence is available where an employer has reasonably attempted to prevent the harassment, or where the individual is hypersensitive. A comparator is unnecessary in harassment cases.

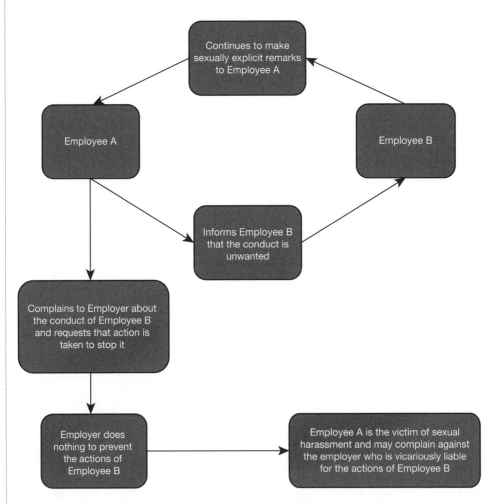

Figure 5.2 Example of the vicarious liability of the employer

Victimisation

Victimisation (for example, intimidation of the individual, unfair pressure, etc.) applies where an individual is subjected to a detriment on the basis that they have performed, or the employer believes they intend to perform what is called a 'protected act'. A protected act, for example, includes initiating proceedings in EA 2010. A comparator is unnecessary in victimisation cases.

Key Definition: Victimisation

This form of prohibited conduct exists where an individual is treated less favourably by an employer as a result of that person either having brought a claim under the Equality Act 2010, their intention to claim, or that they gave evidence at a hearing involving the Act.

Time limits in discrimination cases

The claim for discrimination must be brought within three months of the discriminatory act (or it having ended) although tribunals have the power to extend this time limit where they feel it just and equitable to do so.

In *DeSouza v Manpower UK Ltd* [2012] UKEAT/0234/12/LA, the EAT held that where a claimant is entirely at fault for presenting a claim of race discrimination outside of the limitation period, a tribunal is entitled to decide that it is not just and equitable to extend the period (even, as in this case, by just one day). The claimant had been legally advised of relevant deadlines in which claims had to be lodged at the tribunal service, but due to financial concerns had delayed in proceeding. Where no exceptional reasons for the delay arise, there was no need for the EAT to substitute its own view for that reached by the tribunal.

Remedies

Following a successful finding of discrimination, the three remedies that a tribunal is empowered to award are:

- to declare the rights of the complainant (that they have been the victim of unlawful discrimination, harassment or victimisation);
- to award damages (of which there is no statutory-imposed ceiling and may include the damage suffered to the claimants feelings – even psychiatric injury);

- to make a recommendation that the employer eliminates/reduces the effect of the discrimination for all employees not just the claimant (EA 2010 s. 124).

Injury to feelings

In *Vento v Chief Constable of West Yorkshire* [2003] ICR 318, the Court of Appeal gave broad guidance on the levels of compensation to be awarded in cases of injury to feelings as part of the remedies given following a finding of discrimination. The Court identified three tiers of compensation, although it did note these were to be interpreted as broad and involved considerable flexibility. (1) The most serious cases of discriminatory harassment should involve damages payments of between £15,000–£25,000; (2) serious cases, but those not in the highest band should involve compensation of between £5,000–£15,000; and (3) less serious cases such as one-off incidents should involve damages of between £500–£5,000.

The Court of Appeal (in *Simmons v Castle* [2012] EWCA Civ. 1288) provided guidance on the award of compensation for general damages that took effect from the 1 April 2013. The Court held that the level of general damages in civil cases for pain and suffering; loss of amenity; physical inconvenience and discomfort; social discredit; and mental distress will be '10% higher than previously'. *Simmons* was decided on the basis of personal injury awards, but where injury to feelings applies to instances of discrimination, the increase is likely to be followed.

Age

In 2006 the government provided protection against discriminating against an individual because of their age (Employment Equality (Age) Regulations 2006 SI 2006/1031). Anti-discrimination on the basis of an individual's age is now contained in EA 2010 s. 5, and it protects at all ages, albeit in reality, age discrimination is more likely to be a factor when the individual is a younger worker, or when they are older, and hence closer to retirement. There is no longer a default compulsory retirement age of 65, although direct discrimination on the basis of an individual's age may be lawfully justified by an employer. With regards to indirect age discrimination, as has been identified above, the employer may also lawfully justify such action insofar as there is an objective need for the provision, criterion or practice that has led to the discrimination. Further, this must be a proportionate means to achieve the legitimate aims.

To give an example where age discrimination could be lawfully justified, consider the appointment of fire fighters. This is a job that requires a high level of physical fitness. It may be proportionate to retire a fire fighter at an earlier age than perhaps, a teacher, simply because of this physical requirement. This would have to be justified by the employer, but it does allow an employer to forward the argument for compulsory retirement. Compulsory retirement on the basis of age can be used as a reason for achieving a legitimate aim, such as to encourage younger people into a particular industry, although this has to be justified. The Court of Justice of the European Union held in *EC v Hungary* [2012] Case C286/12 that a compulsory retirement age for judges from 70 to 62 constituted age discrimination. It could not be justified as a proportionate means of achieving legitimate aims. Hungary had attempted to (1) standardise the retirement of professionals in the public sector; and (2) to facilitate a balanced age structure in the profession where younger lawyers could achieve an accelerated career. The lowering of the age of retirement was appropriate for achieving the first aim, although it was not introduced gradually, however, the second aim was not appropriate for the effects, that would only have temporarily established a vacuum in the profession filled by younger lawyers, that would have been achieved. The medium- to long-term effects of the objectives were not going to be met by this aim.

Cost savings as a legitimate aim in discrimination cases

In 2012 the Court of Appeal considered the issue of cost being a 'proportionate means of achieving a legitimate aim' when considering discrimination. In *Woodcock v Cumbria Primary Care Trust* [2012] EWCA Civ. 330, the Trust dismissed Woodcock after a restructuring process, shortly before his 49th birthday, giving him 12 months' notice of his redundancy from the organisation. At the tribunal hearing, it was found that this had been done to ensure Woodcock was dismissed before his 50th birthday because, had he still been employed then, he would have been entitled to a substantial enhanced pension payment. It held that the notice of dismissal was less favourable treatment on the grounds of Woodcock's age. The rule established regarding the argument of 'cost' being a legitimate aim for the purposes of justifying a discrimination claim was identified in *Cross v British Airways* [2005] IRLR 423. 'Cost' could not alone justify a dismissal, but coupled with another reason led to what was known as the 'cost plus' rule which did allow dismissals to be justified. In the EAT, Underhill J was critical of the approach and remarked that it led to game-playing in which the respondent was to 'find the other factor'. The Court of Appeal dismissed Woodcock's appeal and refused permission to appeal to the Supreme Court. In the Court of Appeal, Rimer LJ found that previous domestic and European case authorities resulted in the following questions: was the discrimination a proportionate means of achieving a legitimate aim and, if so, was the treatment complained of such a means? Rimer LJ continued that in the present case, dismissing Woodcock (a redundant employee) was a legitimate aim, and it was further legitimate that they sought to ensure that the dismissal saved the Trust additional costs that would have been incurred. Cost issues are important and are part of substantive questions of proportionality.

Disability

People may suffer discrimination on the basis of a disability they possess, because of society viewing such people as unable to perform particular types of work, or it may be because of perceived costs and inconvenience to an employer in having to make reasonable adjustments to employment. Regardless of any perceived justification of this type of discrimination, to negatively discriminate on the basis of an individual's disability is unlawful. It is also significant to recognise that a person with a disability should not have to request materials to be available to them in a form which they can access, or a building to be made accessible for their needs; it should be the responsibility of the employer or the service provider to have made these provisions without a request being necessary. Importantly, people with disabilities should not be made to feel as though extra or unwanted effort has had to be made to enable them to have access that physically able persons enjoy without thinking.

Disability is included in EA 2010 in s. 6. It identifies a disability as a physical or mental impairment which has a substantial and long-term (will last or is expected to last in excess of 12 months) effect on a person's ability to carry out normal day-to-day activities. In *Leonard v Southern Derbyshire Chamber of Commerce* [2001] IRLR 19, the EAT held that the assessment of day-to-day activities should focus on what the individual could not do, rather than identifying a list of things that they could do. Very importantly, the definition of disability has been extended to include factors such as the diagnosis of cancer, multiple sclerosis and HIV infection. The physical characteristics of these conditions vary significantly, but it is on their diagnosis that protection is provided. Other conditions such as alcoholism or drug addiction are not considered disabilities unless they are the result of the use of medically prescribed drugs, neither are psychological conditions such as voyeurism.

EA 2010 s. 13(3) specifically provides for positive discrimination to be lawful in the case of disability discrimination. Generally, positive discrimination is not a lawful act, if for no other reason than it is simply a mechanism that replaces one form of discrimination with another. There is a debate about whether anti-discrimination legislation should attempt to create equality of outcome (and hence provide a form of positive discrimination) or whether it should pursue a policy of equality of opportunity (which is what most anti-discrimination legislation does), but positive discrimination is lawful only with regards to disability.

It is also very important to recognise that EA 2010 s. 15 prohibits treating a disabled person unfavourably, not less favourably. This is significant in that it removes the need for a disabled person to identify a comparator – a person without the disability – when claiming discrimination.

Where an employer knows of an employee's disability, or should have been aware of the disability, and knew that it was likely to affect the employee in the way they have complained, the employer is under a duty to make 'reasonable adjustments' to avoid the negative effects of the employee's disability affecting their ability to perform the work.

On-the-spot question

? Why is the use of positive action permitted, in an attempt to combat anti-discrimination? How does the distinction between positive action and positive discrimination relate to the theories of equality of outcome v equality of opportunity?

Race

Discrimination based on an individual's race is protected under EA 2010 s. 9 and includes colour, nationality and national/ethnic origins. The issues of colour and nationality are self explanatory, but the issue of national and ethnic origins (including groups) required interpretation from the courts. This led to the important judgment in *Mandla v Dowell Lee* [1983].

Religion or belief

Discrimination against an individual on the basis of their religious or philosophical beliefs, or non-beliefs, is prohibited under EA 2010 s. 10. When reading through s. 10, it is also important to be aware of the Equality and Human Rights Commission (EHRC)'s Code of Practice, which identifies a greater range of protected religions than simply those mainstream religions as provided for in EA 2010. The philosophical beliefs included in EA 2010 are determined on the basis of the facts of each particular case. Guidance as to which factors are indicative of whether a philosophy falls within the remit of s.10 was provided by the EAT in *Grainger plc and ors v Nicholson* [2010] ICR 360.

The protection against discrimination on the basis of religion or belief demonstrates the wider protection of people's rights through the European Convention on Human Rights. It is important to recognise that when dealing with discrimination issues, there exist domestic rights and rights derived from our membership of the EU, and from the UK being a signatory to the European Convention and thereby subject to rulings from the ECHR (see Chapter 2).

KEY CASE ANALYSIS: *Mandla v Dowell Lee* [1983] ICR 385 HL

Background

- The headmaster of a private school refused to admit, as a pupil, a boy who was an orthodox Sikh unless he agreed to remove his turban and cut his hair.
- Wearing of a turban was a manifestation of the boy's ethnic origins.
- The headmaster's reason for the refusal was that the school was based on the Christian faith, and wearing of a turban would accentuate religious and social distinctions. This is something the headmaster wished avoid.
- The boy's father sought a declaration that to refuse his admission to the school constituted on lawful discrimination under the Race Relations Act 1976.
- The County Court held that Sikhs were not a 'racial group' for the purposes of the legislation, and hence the claim was dismissed. An appeal (ultimately to the House of Lords) was made on the basis of whether Sikhs were to be defined as a racial group.

Principle established

- The House of Lords allowed the appeal. It identified that the word 'ethnic' for these purposes, was to be construed widely in a broad cultural and historic sense.
- Factors which demonstrated that a group could be called an 'ethnic group' included that day had a long, shared history distinguishing it from other groups (such as between Sikhs and Punjabis); and it had a cultural tradition of its own, including family and social customs and manners, but not necessarily associated with religious observance.
- Sikhs are a racial group and the rule forbidding boys to wear turbans would not be upheld as it was not justifiable in all circumstances.

The ECtHR decided to balance the ability of an individual to leave their current employment to remove any interference with their right, with the restriction (such as the policy imposed by the employer) and whether it was a proportionate response. This led to the decisions above and shows a more modern (and perhaps enlightened) approach taken by the ECtHR in instances of religious discrimination. It also highlights that such instances of indirect discrimination are very fact specific.

KEY CASE ANALYSIS: *Eweida & Others v UK* **[2013]**
(Applications nos. 48420/10, 59842/10, 51671/10 and 36516/10)

Background

- Article 9 of the European Convention on Human Rights provides the right to freedom of thought, conscience and religion, and a qualified right to manifest one's religion or beliefs. The qualification here is only to the extent that 'such limitations . . . are prescribed by law and are necessary in a democratic society in the interests of public safety, for the protection of public order, health, or morals, or for the protection of the rights and freedoms of others.' The Court revisited the previous approach, which was for affected individuals to leave the employment where they faced interference with their right and find alternative work which did not interfere.
- The following issues were heard by the European Court of Human Rights (ECtHR) in relation to the UK's protection of the ability of employees to manifest their religious beliefs in the workplace:

   1   Ms Eweida was employed by British Airways (BA) and wished to wear a crucifix visible over her uniform in breach of BA's dress code;
   2   Ms Chaplin was a geriatric nurse who also wanted to wear a visible crucifix over her uniform in breach of her employer's dress code;
   3   Ms Ladele was a registrar who was required to perform civil partnership ceremonies and refused due to her beliefs; and
   4   Mr McFarlane was employed to provide counselling services for Relate (an organisation which offers counselling to couples whose relationships are in trouble). He refused to provide sexual counselling for same sex couples.

Principle established

1   BA's uniform policy was designed to establish an 'image' for its members of staff. Given the nature of Ms Eweida's crucifix being discreet and not having any (seemingly) negative impact on the BA brand, the UK had breached Art. 9 by failing to protect Ms Eweida's rights.
2   The balancing act of an individual's right to manifest their religious beliefs versus a right to consider health and safety implications was drawn in Ms Chaplin's case. Interference with her Article 9 rights was necessary due to the nature of her job on a hospital ward.
3 and 4   The cases involving Ms Ladele and Mr McFarlane each involved differences in treatment based on sexual orientation. To justify the differences required a particularly serious reason to be put forward, and while States have a 'wide margin of appreciation' in such cases, this was not exceeded in either case.

Sex and sexual orientation

Discrimination on the basis of an individual's sex applies both to men and women. When, for example, a woman complains of direct discrimination on the basis of her sex, she must compare herself with how a man was or would be treated. Hence, her argument is that she was the victim of detrimental treatment on the basis of her sex.

The comparator used in claims of discrimination does not have to be 'precisely the same' as the claimant. In *Hewage v Grampian Health Board* [2012] UKSC 37 the Supreme Court considered the treatment of a dentist employed at Aberdeen Royal Infirmary. Mrs Hewage argued that as she was a Sri Lankan woman, she had been subject to bullying and harassment. In determining that Hewage had been discriminated against, the Supreme Court referred to the treatment of two white men employed at the Infirmary, including her replacement, who had received cooperation and assistance not made available to Hewage. Even though Hewage's circumstances were not identical to that of the comparators, there existed sufficient similarity to enable a prima facie case of discrimination. The Infirmary had to demonstrate that it had not discriminated against Hewage, which it failed to do.

Discrimination on the basis of an individual's sexual orientation applies to heterosexual, homosexual, and bisexual individuals. The discrimination occurs where an individual is treated less favourably on the basis of this protected characteristic and, particularly in relation to anti-discrimination, on the basis of sexual orientation, the ECtHR had been decisive in outlawing such activities through its interpretation of Article 8 of the ECHR. Further, protection against discrimination on the basis of sexual orientation was sadly lacking in previous anti-discrimination laws from both the UK (Sex Discrimination Act 1975) and the EU (Equal Treatment Directive 1976 76/207/EEC), both of which led to interpretations from the judiciary that sexual orientation was not in their remit. However, the EU Framework Directive specifically provided for protection in this area and led, in 2003, to protection embodied now in EA 2010 s. 12(1).

Gender reassignment

Protection against discrimination of a person who was undergoing, proposing to undergo, or had undergone gender reassignment was outlawed in the Sex Discrimination Act (SDA) 1975. The limitation of the SDA in this regard, was that it identified gender reassignment as a medical process whereby, for example, an individual born a man would undergo medical treatment to live as a woman. The process of undergoing the medical treatment involved in redesigning the individual's gender was particularly onerous and there appeared to be unfairness in this regard. Therefore, EA 2010 provides protection to an individual who decides to live permanently as a person of the opposite gender, regardless of whether that individual undergoes medical treatment to physically alter their gender. Note, however, EA 2010 does not protect individuals (under s. 7) who temporarily live as a person of the opposite gender – for example transvestites.

On-the-spot question

?
 What are the potential difficulties for an employer who operates toilet facilities for employees, and who employs a person born a man who is living permanently as a woman, but who has not undergone a medical process, and who wishes to use toilets designated for women? Consider *Goodwin v UK* [2002] IRLR 664 and the Gender Recognition Act 2004 in your answer.

Marriage and civil partnership

While persons who are married or who have entered into a civil partnership are protected under s. 8 EA 2010, the legislation does not protect single persons (or indeed single parents) or persons who are cohabiting (whether they are an opposite sex couple or same-sex couple). The rights to protection against discrimination on the basis of marriage or civil partnership are quite limited in scope.

Pregnancy and maternity

Women gain protection on the basis of their pregnancy due to the obvious fact that only women become pregnant, and therefore, any act or omission that is detrimental to the woman or her unborn baby, is direct discrimination. The protection begins when the woman becomes pregnant (and procedures exist for women to provide a certificate of pregnancy to an employer to prove that pregnancy – employers must not assume that a woman is in a pregnant state!) and continues until the end of the woman's compulsory maternity leave (for employees, the period of ordinary maternity leave is 26 weeks, with an additional maternity leave period to 52 weeks being applicable where the employee qualifies. For non-employees, the period of protection is two weeks after the end of the pregnancy).

Dismissal of a woman due to her pregnancy is automatically unfair, and an employer may not unreasonably refuse a woman's request to have time away from work to attend antenatal appointments.

An example of law in practice: Let's imagine an employee informs you, as her employer, that she is pregnant. She is supposed to be at her desk at 9am every morning to perform her job. However, over the last two weeks, the employee has not attended work until 10.30am. When you challenge her about this, she informs you that she is suffering from morning sickness and finds it difficult to attend work at 9am. Would it be lawful for you to stop her pay until she attends work at 10.30am, or may you reasonably request that she works through lunch to make up the lost time? Remember, morning sickness is a factor to do with pregnancy. Requiring an employee to come into work at 9am, to work late, to work through a lunch hour/rest period or to dock pay may be seen as a 'detriment' and discrimination. Therefore, a situation to do with requests to attend antenatal care, morning sickness, or general medical conditions due to pregnancy should be handled very sensitively and with full regard to s. 18 EA 2010.

CONCLUSION

As can be seen, discrimination in employment can have devastating effects for the individuals involved and can be very damaging to industrial relations and the reputation of a business. Employers need to be very mindful of the need to follow the law, have effective policies in place to avoid discriminatory conduct, and to take firm action when instances of discrimination occur. This book continues with issues of discrimination as it looks at equal pay between men and women in the next chapter, and it considers the broader aspects of regulation of pay in employment.

FURTHER READING

Vickers, L. and Manfredi, S. (2013) 'Age Equality and Retirement: Squaring the Circle', *Industrial Law Journal*, Vol. 42, No. 1, p.61.
An article reviewing case law authority from domestic and EU courts, and the basis of conclusions on the issue of proportionality in discrimination cases, and balancing the rights of individuals with the needs of businesses.

Pitt, G. (2011) 'Keeping the Faith: Trends and Tensions in Religion or Belief Discrimination', *Industrial Law Journal*, Vol, 40, No. 4, p.384.
A very interesting article looking at the problems this form of anti-discrimination legislation has with regards to the occupational requirement, which is a defence available to a claim of an otherwise discriminatory act.

Anna Lawson, A. (2011) 'Disability and Employment in the Equality Act 2010: Opportunities Seized, Lost and Generated', *Industrial Law Journal*, Vol. 40, No. 4, p.359.
An article which takes a broader view of protection against discrimination on the basis of disability in relation to the United Nations Convention (of which the UK is a signatory) and compares this approach with the other protected characteristics.

www.acas.org.uk/index.aspx?articleid=3017 (ACAS Equality Act Quick Start Guide for Employers).

www.lawsociety.org.uk/productsandservices/practicenotes/equalityact/4556.article (The Law Society: Equality Act – Practice Note for Solicitors).

Chapter 6
Pay

LEARNING OBJECTIVES

After reading this chapter you should be able to:

- explain an employer's duty to provide pay to an employee and where lawful deductions may be made;
- differentiate between wages and expenses;
- identify the national minimum wage applicable and the employer's duty to maintain records of individuals at work;
- explain in what circumstances an individual is entitled to holiday pay and sick pay;
- define the obligation to provide equal pay between men and women, and to identify the 'heads' under which an equal pay claim may be made;
- identify in which circumstances an employer can deviate from paying equal pay between a claimant and that person's comparator.

MIND MAP

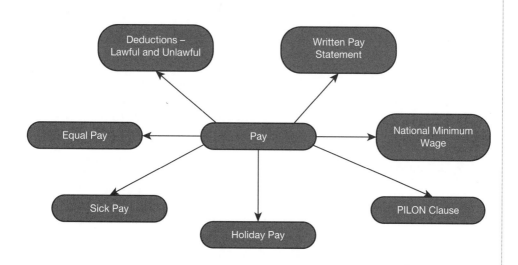

INTRODUCTION

From the outset it is important to recognise an employer's duty to pay wages to an employee. Such an obligation does not necessarily apply to other personnel within a company, such as directors, and the rates of pay and frequency of payments will generally be contained within the contract of employment. Further, the written statement of particulars of employment will also incorporate these details.

Pay includes holiday pay, commission made on earnings, bonuses and all contractual benefits (when looking at an equal pay claim). It does not include expenses incurred by an employee on their employer's business, and therefore you should not just consider pay to be restricted to a term such as 'wages'.

OBLIGATION TO PAY WAGES

The employee's right to receive wages, the amount of wages to be paid, factors such as bonuses, commission payments and so on, and in what intervals (for example, whether weekly or monthly) should be included in the contract of employment. Where these details are missing, it is possible to search for them in the statement of written particulars, evidence such as the advertisement specifications of the job held by the employee, and details must be included in the itemised pay statement to which all employees are entitled. The pay statement is important as it not only identifies the employee's wage, but also information such as National Insurance deductions and any pension contributions.

It is very important to recognise that an employer may not make deductions from the pay provided to an employee unless this is agreed in writing (and consequently is part of the contract of employment), or where the deduction is required through law (for example, National Insurance contributions deducted from the earnings of an employee – see s. 13(1) ERA 1996).

The EAT also held that an employer can commit a fundamental breach of contract by intentionally not paying an employee the full pay owed. In *Roberts v The Governing Body of Whitecross School* [2012] UKEAT/0070/12/ZT it was held that where an employer made an error in payment for an employee who was absent from work due to sickness, the fact that the employer reduced the amount of sick pay due amounted to a fundamental breach of contract which enabled the employee to successfully argue a claim of constructive dismissal.

EXPENSES COMPARED WITH WAGES

In relation to equal pay, expenses are not pay/wages (as provided in the definition in ERA 1996 s. 27(2)(b)). This includes payments made in respect of expenses, such as mileage allowances at work, rather than being restricted to the mere reimbursement of costs incurred for work purposes (see *Quantas v Lopez and Hooper* [2012] UKEAT/0106/12/SM).

DEDUCTIONS FROM PAY

It is possible for an employer to make deductions from the pay received by an individual. Deductions will naturally include elements such as tax and National Insurance contributions as required to be taken from the payments received by employees, and they may also be made where there is an agreement to such deductions as an express term of the contract of employment. ERA 1996 s. 13(2) outlines the requirements to be followed where deductions are to be made in this manner. Essentially, the employer must raise the issue of deductions with the employee and the employee must agree to it. Any unauthorised deductions made by an employer will result in an employee being able to recover the sums. Such unauthorised deductions frequently occur where there is a system of short-time working following a decline in the employer's business (see *IPC Ltd v Balfour* [2003] IRLR 11). In such a scenario, where the employee is performing fewer hours than stipulated in the contract, the employer would pay a reduced wage.

Where an employee claims a deduction in wages has been made by the employer, contrary to the contract of employment, the claim must be lodged at an employment tribunal within three months of the deduction having been made (ERA 1996 s. 23). The tribunal will then be in a position to confirm whether such unlawful deduction was made and, if so, it may award a declaration for the reimbursement of the deducted sum, or what level of deduction was appropriate in the circumstances. A worker adversely affected by such an unlawful deduction may also seek compensation for associated financial losses (ERA 1996 s. 24).

OVERPAYMENT OF WAGES

Where an employer has made an overpayment of wages to an employee, the overpayment may be recovered by the employer only where the overpayment is due to a mistake of fact; the overpayment will not be recoverable where it has been made due to a mistake of law. For example, where an employer had overpaid wages and the employee, knowing that such an incorrect payment has been made, did not bring this to the employer's attention, the employer would be entitled to be reimbursed for the overpayment. However, where an employer had made an overpayment due to a misunderstanding of the National Minimum Wage legislation, these payments would not be recoverable.

NATIONAL MINIMUM WAGE

Workers, not simply those with 'employee' status, are entitled to be paid at the rate set under the National Minimum Wage Act 1998 (updated annually in October). It is important to recognise at this stage that the minimum wage rate does not include pension payments, overtime pay, or expenses, and so on.

The rates depend on the age of the worker (those under the age of 16 do not qualify) and the most recent update is as follows:

Table 6.1 Rates of pay under the National Minimum Wage legislation

Year	21 and over	18 to 20	Under 18	Apprentice
2013 (from 1 October)	£6.31	£5.03	£3.72	£2.68
2012 (current rate)	£6.19	£4.98	£3.68	£2.65
2011	£6.08	£4.98	£3.68	£2.60

An apprentice, for the purposes of the Act, is an individual under the age of 19 or someone in their first year of employment.

The minimum wage is based on the gross pay (that is pay before the deduction of income tax) received by the worker, and this must be subject to a calculation – many people are paid on a monthly basis and their hours at work may vary. Hence it may not be as easy to identify the hourly pay for these individuals as it would be for those individuals employed on a part-time basis. In performing this calculation, the employer may average the hourly pay from the period of work undertaken by the individual, but this average must not exceed one month's work. The employer is also required to maintain records of all payments to workers, including the hours that they worked, and to have these records available for inspection by Her Majesty's Revenue and Customs (HMRC). Where an employer fails to adequately maintain records, they may be subject to prosecution as this, along with falsifying records, is a criminal offence. The employer should also ensure these records are available for inspection by the workers to whom they relate.

The national minimum wage is a statutory requirement, and where employers fail to pay the appropriate amounts, a worker may take action in the civil courts or employment tribunal to enforce their rights. There is also a system of a penalty notice policy where HMRC can enforce the Act, and this may be achieved through a Compliance Officer identifying the sum of money owed to a worker, and the time in which the employer must make payment. Failure to comply with the Act may lead to a fine payable by the employer of up to £5,000.

On-the-spot question

 Do you feel that the system of regulation of the minimum wage is sufficient to ensure compliance? What barriers are in place to adversely affect is usefulness?

STATEMENTS OF PAY

ERA 1996 s. 8 provides that employers are obliged to issue employees, at or before any payment of wages/salary is made, with an itemised pay statement which includes the following information:

> s. 8(2) (a) the gross amount of the wages or salary, (b) the amounts of any variable, and (subject to section 9) any fixed, deductions from that gross amount and the purposes for which they are made, (c) the net amount of wages or salary payable, and (d) where different parts of the net amount are paid in different ways, the amount and method of payment of each part-payment.

Where an employer has not issued the statement of pay as required in s. 8, the employee may claim to an employment tribunal to determine what information should have been provided to the employee. The employee is also entitled to compensation if an employer, having not provided this statement of pay, had made any notified deductions in the preceding 13 weeks. This compensation, however, is limited to an amount not exceeding that of the un-notified deductions (ERA 1996 s. 12(4)).

HOLIDAY PAY

The Working Time Regulations 1998 provide, among other things, the right of an individual to paid holiday each year. Under the current rates, the individual working full-time is entitled to 5.6 weeks' paid leave annually. For those individuals working a 5–day week, this amounts to 28 paid days' holiday. This is the statutory minimum, although many employers offer more generous leave packages, and this will be identified expressly in the contract of employment. One of the reasons why holiday leave is so important, is due to the adverse effects on the individual, and often their performance, where too many consecutive hours have been worked, or insufficient rest has been taken. The Regulations were established through an parent EU Directive, and as such, they apply to those individuals with the status of a 'worker' and not restricted to 'employees'. Those individuals working part-time hours, are also entitled to 5.6 weeks' paid leave, but this will be calculated on the days that they actually work – hence a part-time worker who is engaged three days per week will actually receive 16.8 days of paid leave.

Where a worker has been absent on sick leave, it must be remembered that holiday leave/pay continues to accrue. Article 7 of the EU law – the Working Time Directive 2003/88/EC – and previous judgments of the Court of Justice of the EU (*Stringer v Revenue & Customs* [2009] (Case C-520–06) IRLR 214) each held that annual leave not taken in a year due to illness must be carried over to later in the year or the following year (*Pereda v Madrid Movilidad* [2009] (Case C-227/8)). A period of illness requiring leave is necessary for the recovery to health of the individual. It does not allow the individual to benefit from the rest and recuperation that the Working Time Directive's annual leave provisions are intended to provide. The rolling over of the right to holiday pay does not require that the claimant has requested the payment during the period absent through illness. It is a right that the worker possesses whether or not such a request has been made (see *NHS Leeds v Larner* [2012] EWCA Civ. 1034 and *Georg Neidel v Stadt Frankfurt am Main* [2012] (Case C-337/10)).

SICK PAY

Where an individual is ill and is required to take time off work, there are two principles that must be considered. There may be a contractual right to pay, and there may also be a statutory right to pay – known as statutory sick pay (SSP). Taking the first of these principles, the employer may provide, through the contract of employment, provision for payment of wages during a worker's absence through illness. This is usually performed through an express term in the contract. It is much more difficult to imply such a term unless this is reasonable and there exists evidence that both parties intended for the term to be incorporated in the contract (*Mears v Safecar Security Ltd* [1982] IRLR 183). Where a contract is silent on the issue, it may be useful to refer to a works' handbook, negotiated collective agreement provisions, or evidence of it being the common practice by the employer.

The second principle, payment of SSP, is available to qualifying employees. From the fourth consecutive day of illness, an employee may be entitled to SSP (currently at a rate of £86.70 per week) up to a maximum of 28 weeks, where he or she has earned sufficient wages to pay National Insurance contributions (currently £109 per week) in the previous eight weeks;

has provided the employer with notice of their illness; and, after a seven-day period of illness, has provided the employer with proof.

The Court of Justice of the EU has been active in determining the interpretation and extent of employment rights across a range of issues. It recently considered the rights of workers' access to their annual leave, as provided through the Working Time Directive. The Court of Justice held, in *ANGED v FASGA* [2012] (Case C-78/11) IRLR 779, that where a worker could not access their annual leave accrued during the year of employment (due to the worker's illness), an employer may not replace this period of leave by payment in lieu unless the contract of employment had been terminated.

PAYMENTS IN LIEU OF NOTICE

A payment in lieu of notice (PILON) is a clause that an employer may incorporate into the contract of employment. In the event of the termination of the individual's contract, rather than have the individual work the required notice period, the employer simply pays the employee the money due for the notice period and the individual leaves the employment with immediate effect. As such, PILON is often used in cases of summary dismissal. It is also important to recognise that where a contract of employment expressly allows an employer to make this payment, this would stop a wrongful dismissal (clearly because the employer has complied, technically, with the notice period). Note that these payments, which relate to the termination of employment, are not considered 'pay' as held by the House of Lords in *Delaney v Staples* [1992] 1 AC 687.

Another point in relation to payments in lieu is that, to be effective, such a clause must be expressly contained in the contract. Payment in lieu clauses will not be implied into a contract of employment.

It is also important to distinguish between the type of PILON and whether it will be considered pay. Where an employer provides a PILON as part of what is known as a 'garden leave' arrangement, these payments are pay for the purposes of ERA 1996. A garden leave arrangement is where an employer pays an employee to stay away from the employment, but prevents the employee from working for a competitor or establishing a business potentially in competition with the employer. As there is technically an ongoing relationship with the employer, these payments are deemed wages.

Employers will frequently incorporate a PILON clause to allow for the summary dismissal of an employee. An interesting development of the law occurred in *Cavanagh v William Evans Ltd* [2012] EWCA Civ. 697 where the contract permitted the employer to summarily dismiss the employee where he was issued with six months' PILON. The employer exercised this clause when making the claimant redundant, but it later discovered that the claimant had committed an act of gross misconduct that would have allowed for their dismissal without pay. The employer therefore withheld the payment as required in the contract but the Court of Appeal held that the employer was not entitled to withhold the pay. The contract identified that the claimant was entitled to the payment, there was no clause which provided the employer to deny making the payment, and no principle of contract law which prevented the employee from recovering the pay.

EQUAL PAY

The broader issue of discrimination has been considered in Chapter 5. As identified, most of the previous anti-discrimination legislation was repealed in October 2010 and replaced with EA 2010. This included the provision for equal pay between men and women and is now to be found in ss. 64–70 EA 2010. Further, as equal pay was a protected right under EU law, it is also important to be aware that the United Kingdom must adhere to the Treaty on the Functioning of the European Union Article 157, and judgments of the Court of Justice of the European Union (CJEU). The Treaty and the CJEU have had, and will continue to have, a profound effect on the development and interpretation of this area of law.

Pay, according to the CJEU, involves ALL contractual terms – it is not restricted to wages. Therefore, any contractual provision of remuneration such as wages, occupational pension schemes (see *Barber v Guardian Royal Exchange Assurance Group* [1990] ICR 616), company cars, access to health centres or membership of a gym, discounted mortgage rates, sick pay, redundancy pay, holiday pay and so on are all considered to be paid according to the EU interpretation. This is to prevent any disguised unequal pay between men and women.

Equal pay between men and women

An equality of pay clause is implied into every contract of employment through s. 66 EA 2010. This ensures that, for example, the terms and conditions of a woman's contract are no less favourable than that provided to a man. Where a man's contract includes a benefit not present in that of the contract of a woman, EA 2010 allows the woman's contract to be equalised/modified to incorporate this term (s. 66(2)(b)). Importantly, there are no qualification criteria for this protection, nor do exemptions exist for small businesses. The key criteria here, is that the difference in pay is due to the sex of the claimant and comparator. In some instances men may be paid at a higher rate than women and this will not transgress the requirement of sex equality in pay. Such a situation may be objectively justified by an employer where there is a **material factor** other than sex.

> **Key Definition: Material factor**
>
> Following a prima facia case of unequal pay being established, an employer may present a material factor, other than sex, explaining the difference in pay between the claimant and comparator.

> **Key Definition: Comparator (equal pay)**
>
> To ensure a claim for equal pay may proceed, the claimant must produce a comparator who is receiving higher pay than they are. In most instances an actual comparator is required, however, a hypothetical comparator may be used in cases involving direct gender pay discrimination.

To argue for equality in pay, the claimant first has to produce a **comparator** who, clearly, is receiving higher pay than them, and the claim of equal pay must be on the basis of one of three '**heads' of claim**: like work, work rated as equivalent, or work of equal value.

> **Key Definition: Heads of claim**
>
> The claimant must select a 'head' of claim under which to present their claim for equal pay. The three 'heads' are that the claimant is (1) performing 'like work' with the comparator; (2) performing 'work rated as equivalent' to the comparator; or (3) performing work of 'equal value' to that of the comparator.

The comparator

An equal pay claim necessitates that the claimant is being paid at a lower rate than that received by the comparator, and the reason for the difference in pay relates to their sex. Hence, traditionally the example provided through legislation (the Equal Pay Act (EPA) 1970) was of a woman as a claimant comparing herself with the pay received by a man. EA 2010 has introduced gender neutral examples (using A and B as the claimant and comparator), but it still requires the difference in pay to be between a woman and a man.

In most cases, an actual comparator will be required. This involves an individual who is employed by the same employer, at the same establishment as the claimant, and associated employer, or at an establishment where common terms and conditions are used (for example, where the same collective bargaining unit is in operation – see *Lawrence v Regent Office Care Ltd* [2003] ICR 1092 and s. 79 EA 2010). In *City of Edinburgh Council v Wilkinson* [2010] IRLR 756 the 'same establishment' provision was extended to individuals employed at the Council, regardless of its geographical location.

The comparator may be the predecessor of the claimant (see *Macarthys Ltd v Smith* [1980] IRLR 210), but not the successor to a post vacated by the claimant. Also be aware that since the commencement of EA 2010, a hypothetical comparator may be used in cases involving direct gender pay discrimination.

The three heads of claim

The claimant is required to identify the head under which they wish to bring the claim, and while help may be provided by the tribunal, particularly where the claimant is not represented in a hearing, the decision is for the claimant to choose the most appropriate 'head' in their circumstances.

Like work

The claimant is likely to choose this head of claim where they are performing like or similar work to that of the comparator (s. 65(1)(b) EA 2010). The work does not have to be exactly the same (*Capper Pass Ltd v Lawton* [1977] ICR 83), and minor differences will be ignored. It is also the tribunal's job to identify the actual work being undertaken by the claimant and comparator, not necessarily what is identified in the contract (see *Shields v Coomes (Holdings) Ltd* [1987] ICR 1159).

Work rated as equivalent

An employer may voluntarily undertake a job evaluation study where the roles undertaken by individuals will be objectively assessed, graded, and with pay scales clearly identified. This aids transparency and is frequently undertaken by public sector employers to demonstrate no discrimination between men and women at work. In order for this to be used as an effective defence forwarded by an employer, it has to be demonstrated that the study was appropriate, objective and was not a 'smokescreen' facilitating discriminatory practices.

For an employer to be able to rely on this head to defeat an equal pay claim, the study must be analytical; objectively assessed; the claimant's and comparator's jobs must have formed part of the study; and the study must have been conducted at the place of employment where the claimant worked.

Work of equal value

To ensure the requirements of EU law were met and that men and women were paid without discrimination based on their sex, the 'head' of equal value was incorporated into the legislation. This allows the claimant and comparator to be employed in different roles, yet the work each performs for the employer adds the same value. This was an important development as traditionally there are occupations predominantly performed by women and others predominantly performed by men. Without this head of claim, equal pay would have been even more difficult to achieve than currently exists. Equal value refers to factors such as effort, skill and decision-making, and the employer must not attempt to equalise pay between men and women with regards to broad aspects of the contract (see Figure 6.1). Each term and condition of the contract must be equal in this calculation.

Material factors

Where the claimant's argument that they have received unequal pay has been satisfied, the burden is then placed on the employer to justify, if the employer can, that the reason for the difference in pay is not due to sex (a material factor – s. 69 EA 2010). This requires the employer to objectively justify (therefore it must not be a discriminatory exercise) a difference in pay between that of the claimant and the comparator as being the consequence of a business need, and that the actions of the employer were a 'proportionate means' of achieving this aim. Examples of material factors include:

Market forces

An employer may have to pay some individuals a higher rate of pay to meet the current market value or to reflect a shortage in supply of the services provided by the individual. For example, where individuals are recruited from the private sector to take jobs in the public sector, it may be necessary to pay those recruited in such a manner the current market rate to encourage those to leave the private sector. If the current public sector workers are mainly women, and the individuals recruited from the private sector are mainly men, any difference in pay can be justified on the basis of the recruitment exercise and the need to entice individuals into the public sector (where generally pay rates are lower than the private sector). Hence, the difference in pay is not sex but the nature of the market from where individuals have been recruited (see *Rainey v Greater Glasgow Health Board* [1987] IRLR 26).

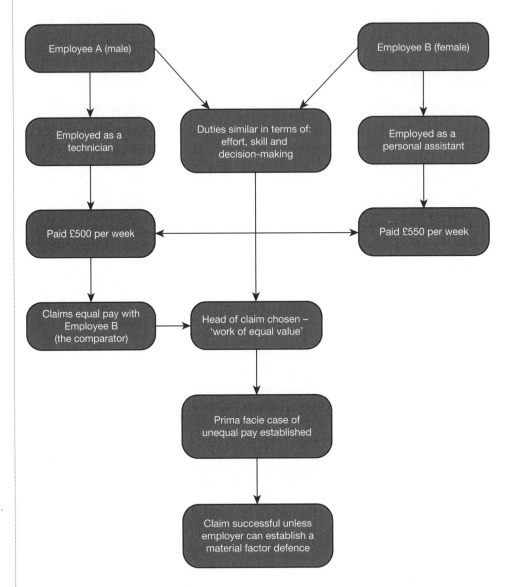

Figure 6.1 Equal pay example

Experience

Seniority in employment is generally rewarded with incremental pay increases. This has been justified on the basis of rewarding loyalty and reflecting experience. Where men with greater experience are paid a higher rate than women with less experience, this may be justified by the employer.

KEY CASE ANALYSIS: *Hayward v Cammell Laird Shipbuilders* **[1988] IRLR 257**

Background

- The claimant (a woman) was employed as a cook.
- The comparators used were men employed in occupations including joinery, engineering, and painting.
- The employer admitted paying the claimant and comparators differently, but argued that when viewed as a whole, the claimant's contract was no less favourable than that of the comparators.

Principle established

- The House of Lords held that each term of the claimant's contract had to be as favourable as those enjoyed by the comparator(s).
- It was contrary to the relevant legislation to attempt to equalise contracts as a whole.
- Equal pay had to be provided and any discrimination could only be justified on the basis of a material difference between the claimant and comparator – not their sex.

Regions

Equal pay claims may be made by individuals engaged by the employer or associated employer. As such, claims may be made by the claimant employed in one region of the country, and the comparator engaged by the same employer (albeit at a different workplace) in a different part of the country. As pay rates can differ, particularly in England where there is a north/south divide in wages paid, this regional variation may be justified as a difference in pay between the claimant and comparator (see *NAAFI v Varley* [1976] IRLR 408).

With each of the material factor defences identified above (a non-exhaustive list), this does not necessarily mean the employer will avoid a finding of unequal pay. Rather, it acts as a means for an employer to justify that a difference in pay affecting men and women was not in fact due to their sex, but was for some objective and (potentially) justifiable business reason.

Time limits for claims

An equal pay claim may be made at any time during which the individual is employed under what is known as a 'stable employment relationship' (see *Preston v Wolverhampton Healthcare NHS Trust* [2001] UKHL 5). There may, of course, be potential problems between an employer and individual where an equal pay claim is made during the employment relationship. As such, an individual may wait until the employment relationship has come to an end and then bring a 'rolled-up' claim (back-dated for up to six years) within six months of the termination of the employment contract. This six-month period may be extended where an employer has deliberately misled the individual as to their rights, or where the individual is suffering a disability that has prevented the claim being made. The six-month time limit to bring a claim will generally run from the time from when the individual left the employment, although in *Foley v NHS Greater Glasgow & Clyde* [2012] UKEATS/0008/12/BI, the EAT held that it also applies to the dissolution (winding-up) of an organisation.

Equal pay and breach of contract

As explained above, the time limit for claims of equal pay is six months. In *Birmingham City Council v Abdulla* [2011] EWCA Civ. 1412, the Court of Appeal considered the availability of an equal pay claim through the civil courts. Former employees of the Council, totalling 174 individuals, claimed that a refusal to grant the female claimants equal pay with various comparator groups amounted to a breach of contract. The Council argued that the civil court should strike out the claim as it was (by the time the claim was brought in the civil court) after the six-month time limit imposed by the statute for such claims. The Court of Appeal upheld the decision of the High Court to dismiss the Council's application and explained that while EPA 1970, s. 2(3) (now incorporated into EA 2010 s. 122) provided discretion in striking out claims which could be more conveniently be determined in an employment tribunal, it would amount to extreme judicial discretion to strike out a claim for breach of the Act which was lodged within the limitation period for the civil courts (six years). Parliament had provided claimants with two routes in which to commence proceedings and the claimants did not have to provide an explanation as to their choice. In [2012] UKSC 47, the Supreme Court upheld (3–2) the decision and determined that employees could essentially circumvent the time limit for equal pay claims applicable to the employment tribunal through claiming in the civil courts.

It is important to note that the Supreme Court did warn that where a claimant had deliberately delayed in lodging a claim in the employment tribunal to gain an 'illegitimate advantage' by bringing a claim in the civil courts, they risked having the claim struck out because of an abuse of process, and further that where the claimant should, reasonably, have claimed in the tribunal, this should be considered in the award of costs.

On-the-spot question

 Given that equal pay legislation has been in force for nearly 40 years, what are the reasons for the continued disparity in pay between men and women?

CONCLUSION

Having considered the important issue of pay when working, the next chapter begins the consideration of another vital issue in employment law, the termination of the contract and ending the relationship. Wrongfully and unfairly dismissing an individual can be a very expensive and damaging action for the employer, and personally devastating to the individual. Knowledge of this area of law is vital to your understanding of employment law.

FURTHER READING

Fredman, S. (2008) 'Reforming Equal Pay Laws', *Industrial Law Journal*, Vol. 37, p. 193.
The article presents an argument for the reform of the equal pay law which has had a limited effect on pay disparity between men and women.

Steele, I. (2010) 'Sex Discrimination and the Material Factor Defence under the Equal Pay Act 1970 and the Equality Act 2010', *Industrial Law Journal*, Vol. 39, p. 264.
A very informative article addressing the problem of ensuring the domestic law on equal pay was compatible with the ever advancing EU law.

Chapter 7
Termination of the contract of employment: wrongful dismissal

LEARNING OUTCOMES

Having read this chapter you should be in a position to:

- identify the notice period required at common law for termination of the contract for any reason;
- identify the statutory-imposed minimum notice periods for termination of the employment contract;
- explain how dismissal without notice (summary dismissal) can be justified in the event of the worker committing a fundamental breach of the contract;
- explain how evidence discovered after the dismissal is admitted by the courts and may be used to make lawful an otherwise wrongful dismissal;
- identify that the primary remedy in wrongful dismissal claims is damages, although injunctions are used to protect the parties' interests.

INTRODUCTION

Contracts of employment are contracts of personal service. As with any contract or any relationship, at some point it will end. This may be because of some significant disagreement between the parties, it could be that a particular project for which the parties began their relationship has been concluded, or indeed one of the parties may simply decide that they no longer wish to be in the relationship. Therefore, whenever the employment relationship comes to an end, this may involve performance of the contract, a dismissal, a mutual agreement to release each other from further contractual obligations, or a resignation by the individual.

At this stage it is important to recognise that while an individual may qualify to bring a claim for either **wrongful dismissal** of unfair dismissal, that is no indication of the likely success. When dealing with termination of the employment relationship, the first stage is to identify to which right the individual qualifies, then assess which remedy the individual wishes to pursue, and then identify the likely success of each. This will help you in advising an individual, whether this is in a problem-type question set in some university assessment, or whether you are advising a client.

MIND MAP

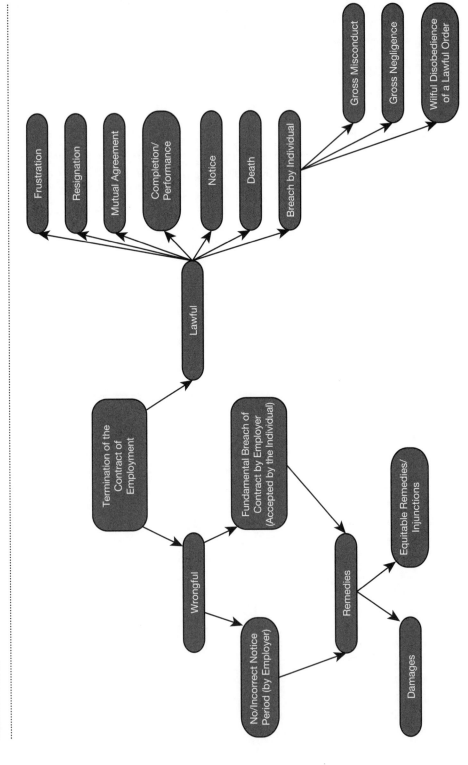

Key Definition: Wrongful dismissal

A dismissal in breach of the contract of employment, most commonly seen when a worker is unjustifiably dismissed contrary to the required notice period.

TERMINATING THE CONTRACT

There exist several reasons for the termination of the contract of employment. The contract may become frustrated due to its becoming radically different from that which was envisaged when the engagement began, or because the contract subsequent to the agreement becomes impossible to perform. The parties may wish to end the contract through mutual agreement, or the employer may wish to terminate the contract through providing the individual with correct notice. Further, the individual may choose to leave the employment and seek opportunities elsewhere by providing the employer with their resignation. And finally, and very important to this chapter, the contract could be terminated through dismissal. Unlike unfair dismissal, dismissal at common law is not subject to the same procedural rules that must be followed in order to lawfully dismiss an individual. It is based on the principles of contract law. The main forms of dismissal are:

- **summary dismissal** (no notice given / 'on the spot' sacking);
- wrongful dismissal (essentially a breach of contract);
- unfair dismissal (a dismissal contrary to statutory protection);
- **constructive dismissal** (an unfair dismissal claim lacking a dismissal – a fundamental breach of contract accepted by the employee).

The first two examples are considered in this chapter. The latter two are covered in Chapter 8.

Key Definition: Summary dismissal

A dismissal without notice – perhaps referred to as being 'sacked on the spot'. Essentially, the employer has not conducted any investigation before deciding to dismiss. Such dismissals can be justified (lawful) or unjustified (wrongful).

> ### Key Definition: Constructive dismissal
>
> A resignation by the individual in response to an employer's fundamental breach of the contract. It enables the individual to seek a remedy under wrongful and/or unfair dismissal.

Termination through frustration

Contract law allows for the parties to be released from further obligations under the contract, without fault being apportioned, where the contract becomes radically/fundamentally different from that which was agreed; or whether the contract becomes impossible to perform, and this was the fault of neither party. Unless provided for in the contract, the law regulating frustration is the Law Reform (Frustrated Contracts) Act 1943.

Examples of frustration include: illness (*Condor v Baron Knights* [1966] 1WLR 87), due to an injury sustained by the worker (*GF Sharp & Co Ltd v McMillan* [1998] IRLR 632); and imprisonment where a significant proportion of the contract cannot be performed (*F.C. Shepherd & Co. Ltd. v Jerrom* [1986] IRLR 358). This remains a 'doctrine of last resort' and will not be easily granted by the courts (*Williams v Watson Luxury Coaches Ltd* [1990] IRLR 164).

Termination through mutual agreement

The employer and the individual may agree to bring the contract of employment to an end (see *Martin v MBS Fastenings (Glynwed) Distribution Ltd* [1983] IRLR 198 regarding 'genuine' mutual agreement). This is known as mutual agreement and the act of the employer not requiring the individual to work a contractually required notice period, and the corresponding act of the individual not seeking compensation for termination from the employer amounts to 'consideration' in contract law to make such an agreement legally binding between the parties. Such examples may be seen in which an employer seeks voluntary severance (although usually there is monetary compensation involved to encourage individuals to leave the employment early) or where the manager of a professional sports team has a difference of opinion with the owners and each release the other from any further action on the contract. Where the parties mutually agree to release each other from the contract, and given that the individual will consequently have no claim for compensation, the courts and tribunals will look for some outward sign of inducement in establishing the genuine nature of a 'mutual' agreement.

Termination through resignation/notice

An individual is entitled to provide the employer with his/her notice of the intention to resign and leave employment. The notice period required is often contained in the statement of written particulars, or with reference to ERA 1996, s. 86. It is also not uncommon for an employer not to hold the individual to work the notice period where it is convenient for the individual to leave employment immediately. The general position is that an individual who provides his/her employer with notice is not entitled to compensation. However, note the possibility of a claim for compensation where the resignation has been submitted and the individual intends to claim constructive dismissal.

Employers, under the common law, are required to provide a notice period when choosing to terminate the contract of employment. The reason for the employer's choice of termination is of no consequence. They are entitled to dismiss for whatever reason insofar as the correct notice period is provided. This further raises the issue that simply because a dismissal is lawful at common law, that does not prevent the individual from seeking a remedy through unfair dismissal (if the individual qualifies and the employer's action is contrary to law).

The requirement for the individual to provide the correct notice is to protect the parties. Without the correct notice period being served, the employer may face difficulties in staffing and adherence to contractual obligations that they have with third parties. This also works in exactly the same way with the protection afforded to individuals. Under the common law, an employer is also entitled to terminate the contract of employment through providing the individual with the correct notice period (and if the contract provides, to issue a PILON rather than requiring the individual to work the notice period).

In the event that either party fails to provide the correct notice period, the innocent party may seek to recover damages for any losses incurred. For the employer, this may be limited to wages provided to another person to cover the individual's breach of contract. It is unlikely that an employer would recover any sums for difficulties in meeting contractual obligations (generally because no such losses would have been incurred or could be quantified as a result of this individual's actions) unless the individual was a member of, for example, senior management within the organisation, an individual in the entertainment or sports industries, etc. Where an employer would have power, is in not providing a reference to an individual who has left employment without providing the correct notice period, or identifying this clearly in any reference provided. It is also worthy of note that an employer, even when faced with an individual resigning in breach of contract, may not withhold holiday pay or accrued wages as such action will be considered an unlawful deduction (see Chapter 3) unless this is provided for through express agreement between the parties.

An important issue to remember is that an individual's resignation requires a voluntary act. Where the individual has been 'encouraged' to resign through a threat of dismissal or discipline unless they resign, the courts have held this will not be a true and genuine resignation. It will enable the individual to subsequently seek damages for dismissal if they so choose (*Logan-Salton v Durham County Council* [1989] IRLR 99).

NOTICE PERIODS

It is always advisable, to ensure certainty between the parties, for the contract of employment to clearly identify the notice period required for the termination of the contract. Contracts may provide a definite period for employment – a fixed-term contract. At the end of the fixed term, the contract is ended and both parties are released from further obligations. When the contract is terminated on the conclusion of a fixed-term contract, there is no breach of contract if it is not renewed (there is no claim for wrongful dismissal). However, this does not mean that there is no claim for unfair dismissal, and you should remember that non-renewal of a fixed-term contract will enable a claim for unfair dismissal. The employer need then justify why the contract is not to be renewed.

The notice period does not have to be the same for the employer and the individual. The minimum notice period gives both parties protection to find a replacement where the other decides to terminate the relationship. Notice periods cannot be excessively long, nor can they be below the minimum periods identified in ERA 1996 s. 86. Section 86 gives the minimum notice periods applicable for termination of the contract of employment (where the employer has no reasonable reason to end the contract in a shorter period of time). Table 7.1 demonstrates the period of employment and the minimum period of notice required for a lawful dismissal.

Table 7.1 Notice periods in termination of the contract

Period of employment	Required notice period
Less than one month	None
More than one month but less than 2 years	1 week
More than 2 years but less than 12 years	Maximum of 12 weeks (one week for every year worked)
More than 12 years	12 weeks

MITIGATION

Where the employer terminates the contract of employment in breach of the required notice period, this will form the basis of a damages claim for wrongful dismissal. Unless the employer has a reason for termination without notice (such as the individual having committed an act of gross misconduct or gross negligence), the individual is entitled to seek recovery of these losses. Remember, this is a claim for breach of contract (albeit a contract of employment) and the individual will have to quantify their losses and have sought mitigation.

Having suffered a wrongful dismissal the injured party must take reasonable steps to avoid further damages accruing. This does not require the affected individual to accept any job that is offered to them, or to take up employment at a much lower level than had been enjoyed while employed. It does, however, require that the individual has attempted (reasonably) to minimise the adverse effects of the employer's breach of contract. The rationale for this obligation is due to public policy and the very negative effects that would have been the consequence of allowing an injured party to sit back and allow losses to

KEY CASE ANALYSIS: *Brace v Calder* [1895] 2 QB 253

Background

- Mr Brace was employed by Calder, Scotch whiskey merchants comprising of four partners.
- Having agreed a contract to serve as the managing director of the firm for two years, five months later Brace was informed that two of the partners were to retire.
- Brace was offered to continue in his present role, albeit serving two partners instead of four.
- Brace refused, resigned and claimed wrongful dismissal.

Principle established

- The Court of Appeal held that the disillusion of the partnership (where two partners left before the end of the contract) resulted in the contract that Mr Brace had agreed being breached.
- Brace was entitled to accept this repudiation.
- However, Brace had acted unreasonably in not accepting the suitable offer of employment by the two remaining partners, and as a consequence was awarded nominal damages of £50.

accrue without any responsibility imposed on them to seek alternative employment and negate the consequential losses. Typically, this will involve the respondent employer enquiring from the claimant details of which jobs have been applied for since the dismissal, any offers of employment, and if such offers have not been accepted, justifiable reasons explaining why.

A further element of interest in mitigation is not only the issue of applying for, and accepting offers of alternative employment, but also, as in *Konczac v BAE Systems (Operations) Ltd* [2012] UKEAT/0498/11/DM where the EAT held that a claimant who refused to accept an offer of settlement failed to the duty to mitigate.

Limitations to the extent of reasonably mitigating losses was highlighted in the EAT in *F & G Cleaners Ltd v Saddington* [2012] UKEAT/0140/11/JOJ where three employees were dismissed following a Transfer of Undertakings (Protection of Employment) (TUPE) Regulations 2006 transfer. The new employer refused to accept that the claimants were employees but offered them re-employment in the same roles as they previously held with the former employer, but on a self-employed basis. The new contract also offered them inferior terms including lower earnings. The claimants refused to accept the re-employment, and the EAT held that they were entitled to reject this offer and had not failed to mitigate their losses. The EAT further provided that in similar circumstances, where an employee refused to accept re-employment on the basis of self-employment instead of as an employee, and the only evidence for an inferior contract was the loss of the protection against unfair dismissal, such a refusal to accept the contract could amount to a failure to mitigate.

Termination by dismissal

The next chapter considers the statutory protection against unfair dismissal. This right was established in 1971 and a further protection to employees than was available under the common law. The employment relationship, remember, is a contract of employment and therefore must adhere to the general principles of contract law. This identifies the terms – whether express or implied – details regarding the nature of employment and the parties' rights and obligations, and it will also identify mechanisms to end the relationship. Some of these details will be proscribed by law, while others are open to the parties to decide. Contract law, then, provides for lawful mechanisms for ending the employment relationship. Where the terms of the contract have been adhered to, the employment relationship, as with any other contract, may be terminated at either party's request.

An employer may also choose to terminate a contract of employment without providing the notice period (and payment during this time or by making a PILON) where the individual has breached some fundamental term through, for example, an act of gross misconduct or gross negligence, and the employer accepts this act as a repudiatory (fundamental) breach of contract. Termination of the contract without providing the required notice period is called a summary dismissal, essentially the employer terminates the contract with immediate effect. The key issue to remember with a summary dismissal is that, in adhering to contract principles, where there is a fundamental breach of the contract (this would be a breach of a condition, rather than of a warranty) the innocent party (here it would be the employer) is entitled to accept the breach, claim damages (where appropriate) and end the contract. It is important for the employer, therefore, to identify the breach as a fundamental element of the contract. Where it is a lesser term (and the difficulty exists in defining which elements of the contract are necessarily fundamental) the employer is not entitled to dismiss without notice. However, employers may still dismiss an individual in such circumstances, but will have to follow a disciplinary procedure to justify the reason – see *Lowndes v Specialist Heavy Engineering Ltd* [1976] IRLR 246.

Justifying a summary dismissal

While there is no guarantee or certainty in relation to what constitutes a gross misconduct, employers are increasingly identifying acts and omissions in documents such as the contract of employment or a works handbook, which give examples of activities that will constitute gross misconduct. This not only includes elements such as theft, violence at work, gross forms of insubordination, but it also reflects the modern world and activities through social media.

Table 7.2 identifies examples (but this is not an exhaustive list) of activities that have been held by the courts to constitute gross misconduct/negligence and to justify a summary dismissal:

Note that it is not uncommon for the reasons for dismissal to overlap and this table has artificially separated the reasons to assist in providing you with example behaviour.

Two cases that demonstrate the approaches taken to gross misconduct involve gardeners.

Table 7.2 Justifying summary dismissal

Act or omission	Example	Case example
Wilful disobedience of a lawful order	A serious defiance of authority, even where the employer genuinely, but mistakenly, believes they are entitled to require the individual to comply with a lawful order	*Farrant v Woodroffe School* [1998] IRLR 176
Misconduct	This can be in connection with the business or outside it if sufficiently grave (e.g. criminal activities)	*Creffield v The BBC* [1975] IRLR 23
Dishonesty	Stealing, fraud, unfair use/collection of confidential company information	*Faccenda Chicken Ltd v Fowler* [1986] 1 All ER 617
Incompetence or neglect	Individuals should use skills they profess to have, but note the overlap with misconduct	*Dietman v Brent LBC* [1987] IRLR 259
Gross negligence	Negligently landing a passenger plane	*Taylor v Alidair* [1978] IRLR 82
Lying to employer	Claiming time away from work due to illness – employer is entitled to go 'behind' any evidence provided by the individual	*Hutchinson v Enfield Rolling Mills* [1981] IRLR 318
Drunkenness	If this occurs when driving a vehicle it undermines the confidence of the employer and/or third parties	*H B Raylor & Co Ltd v McCardle* (1985) EAT 573/84
Gross misconduct	Insolent and disobedient actions of a sufficiently serious extent.	*Pepper v Webb* [1969] 2 All ER 216

KEY CASE ANALYSIS: *Pepper v Webb* [1969] 2 All ER 216

Background

- Pepper was employed as a gardener who had been employed for three months and who had, prior to the dismissal, been held in good regard by the employer.
- On the day of his dismissal, the employer's wife was in charge of Pepper's duties.
- A personality clash between Pepper and the employer's wife led to a reduction in his performance and attitude.
- On Saturday, Pepper was due to finish work when he was instructed to continue planting in a greenhouse.

- Pepper refused and remarked 'I couldn't care less about your bloody greenhouse and your sodding garden.'
- Pepper was summarily dismissed for gross misconduct.

Principle established

- The actions of the employee, including the recent evidence of unsatisfactory behaviour, justified a summary dismissal.
- Pepper's act was the 'last straw' which enabled the employer to accept his action as gross misconduct.

On-the-spot question

 Why did the Court not consider the issue of lawful and reasonable orders, and the fact that undertaking the work would have extended Pepper's working hours when providing its judgment?

KEY CASE ANALYSIS: *Wilson v Racher* [1974] IRLR 114

Background

- Wilson was employed as a gardener and had been involved in cutting a hedge in the garden using electric hedge trimmers.
- Wilson stopped this activity during a rainstorm due to the nature of using electric equipment and the dangers it would present.
- Wilson was criticised by his employer for stopping work, where an argument ensued.
- At the most heated point of the argument, Wilson swore at his employer and was summarily dismissed.

Principle established

- The Court of Appeal held that the dismissal was wrongful.
- Wilson had been an employee of very high standing and his reaction by swearing was merely in response to the employer's unjust accusations and provocation.
- *Wilson* was decided at a time when the courts had been moving away from the previous 'master and servant' concept of employment relations, to one underpinned by mutual respect (trust and confidence)

REMEDIES

A wrongful dismissal is a breach of contract. It simply means that the terms of the contract of employment have been breached and the innocent party, here it will be the individual, has the option to pursue a remedy through the civil courts. The general remedy for a wrongful dismissal is a common law damages claim, although equitable remedies such as injunctions have been awarded by the courts, and there is nothing, in theory at least, to prevent the award of the remedy of specific performance.

Damages

A breach of contract claim (wrongful dismissal) involves the award of damages, but these are limited to the financial loss applicable during the contractual notice period. This can be relatively low (see *Smith v Trafford Housing Trust* [2012] EWHC 3221 (Ch.) where a wrongful dismissal – in the form of a demotion at work – resulted in the claimant being awarded £98). The *Smith* case is also interesting as it further identifies the importance of bringing a claim in time and in the most appropriate tribunal. Smith had argued that he had been unfairly dismissed, but the High Court held that his contract was terminated when he agreed to work in a different capacity for the employer. Hence his claim was of wrongful dismissal.

Damages awarded include the following elements:

- Loss, including 'injury to feelings' but not in cases of unfair dismissal (*Edwards v Chesterfield Royal Hospital NHS Trust* [2011] UKSC 58).
- Lost wages due on the balance of the contract (on a fixed-term contract), or for the wages owed for the notice period required (either in the contract or as required by ERA 1996 s. 86) – *Addis v Gramophone Co. Ltd.* [1909] AC 488.
- Any contractual benefits due in the period of the notice/balance of the fixed-term contract.
- Losses associated with the dismissal (breaches of the contract in the lead up to the dismissal).
- Losses sustained in the aftermath of the dismissal – such as obtaining alternative employment. This is often referred to as 'stigma damages' following *Malik v Bank of Credit and Commerce International SA (in liquidation)* [1997] 3 All ER 1 but this was an exceptional case involving exceptional circumstances. It does not create a general rule for an individual to claim damages where he/she cannot obtain employment following a dismissal.
- As wrongful dismissal is a breach by the employer of an individual's contract of employment, the at-fault employer cannot seek to enforce contractual terms such as invoking a restraint of trade clause.

Injunctions

As wrongful dismissal involves breach of contract, the common law remedy and the equitable remedies are available to the courts. Remember, being equitable remedies, they are available at the court's discretion and will only be awarded where damages will not adequately compensate the injured party. The use of injunctions is possible to prevent a party from breaching their contract (*Warner Bros. v Nelson* [1936] 3 All ER 160), but the remedy of specific performance will not be awarded in an attempt to compel an individual to undertake work as part of contractual duties. It may be used to compel a party to perform a specific element of the contract, but this would not be appropriate for a contract of personal service where the aim was to contract the individual to work. This would be a practical impossibility.

The case that established the availability of equitable remedies (despite the ruling provided in *Ridge v Baldwin* [1964] AC 40) was *Hill v CA Parsons & Co.* [1972] Ch. 305 involving an employer dismissing an employee, contrary to the contractual dismissal procedures, due to pressure by a trade union. The Court of Appeal identified key criteria, listed below, to be satisfied where an injunction would be an appropriate remedy in cases of wrongful dismissal. This was approved in *Irani v Southampton and South West Hampshire Health Authority* [1985] IRLR 203 where a doctor was dismissed contrary to agreed procedures when he and his superior had irreconcilable differences at work. Being the junior member of staff, Irani was dismissed.

1   there must still exist between the parties mutual trust and confidence so that the employment relationship has not irreconcilably broken down;
2   the claimant must seek protection of statutory rights (in this case the grievance procedure that was applicable to the Health Service); and
3   damages would not be an adequate remedy in the case. Here, had Mr Irani been dismissed it was unlikely that he would have been able to work in the Health Service again.

Judicial review

Servants of the Crown (e.g. senior managers in the public sector and senior civil servants) have, generally and traditionally, been held as 'office holders' rather than employees. As such, they are subject not to private law (and therefore wrongful and unfair dismissal), but rather they are subject to public law – the law between the individual and the state. In the circumstance that an individual who is an office holder is dismissed, he/she may seek to challenge the validity of the decision through judicial review. An example of this remedy being used is in *Ridge v Baldwin* where the Chief Constable claimant sought to have his dismissal declared null and void on the basis that the decision was contrary to the principles of natural justice.

To recap, following a finding of wrongful dismissal, the employee may claim:

1 damages, as the standard remedy (*Addis v Gramophone Co Ltd* [1909]);
2 damage to reputation (but very case-specific – see *Malik v Bank of Credit and Commerce International* [1997]);
3 an injunction to force the employer to comply with contractual disciplinary/dismissal procedures (*Irani v South West Hampshire Health Authority* [1985]);
4 a judicial review of a decision to dismiss (*Ridge v Baldwin*).

WHY CLAIM WRONGFUL DISMISSAL?

Many assessment questions will involve dismissals generally. While the question may use unfair dismissal and wrongful dismissal as discrete example topics, it is not uncommon that the (problem-based) question can involve both areas and it will be for you to determine, and in your advice to the parties, explain which route is most appropriate. This type of question has many facets, but ultimately it may come down to what is the most appropriate remedy. Whenever you are answering examination or assessment questions, always consider whether the parties qualify for unfair and wrongful dismissal, and take into consideration the following points:

- hearings are heard in an employment tribunal (where the damages sought are under £25,000); or in the County Court and High Court (where Legal Aid is possible);
- ordinary appeals are available;
- claims must be lodged within six years (Limitation Act 1980);
- no employee status is required;
- no qualifying period is imposed;
- no upper amount for compensation is imposed (it is based on the contract). As such it is:
  (i) particularly attractive for fixed-term contracts with no early termination clause (e.g. professional sports managers); and
  (ii) can be better for higher earners than unfair dismissal (*O'Laoire v Jackel International* [1990] IRLR 170).

CONCLUSION

The common law remedy of wrongful dismissal provides an effective mechanism for redress for individuals whose dismissal conflicts with the terms of their contract. Parliament created further rights for individuals with the employment status of employee through a route of unfair dismissal. This remedy is the focus of the next chapter but ensure that you understand the differences, particularly in relation to qualification and the remedy is involved, of these two routes.

FURTHER READING

Collins, H. (2012) 'Compensation for Dismissal: In Search of Principle', *Industrial Law Journal*, Vol. 41, No. 2, p. 208.
An evaluation of the concept of compensation, and it limitations, in cases of dismissal – comparing the models adopted for the common law of wrongful dismissal, and unfair dismissal, which follows a torts-like measure.

Ewing, K. D. (1993) 'Remedies for Breach of the Contract of Employment', *Cambridge Law Journal*, Vol. 52, p. 405.
The paper explains the use of the equitable remedy of injunctions and the principles of quantifying damages in common law.

Chapter 8
Termination of the contract of employment: unfair and constructive dismissal

LEARNING OBJECTIVES

After reading this chapter you should be able to:

- identify the qualification criteria necessary to bring an unfair dismissal claim;
- explain the potentially fair reasons for the dismissal of an employee;
- critique the reasonableness of an employer's decision to dismiss an employee;
- explain the substantive and procedural elements to unfair dismissal;
- explain the available remedies for unfair dismissal;
- determine the main differences between an action for wrongful dismissal and unfair dismissal, and identify which is the more appropriate action in the individual's circumstance.

MIND MAP

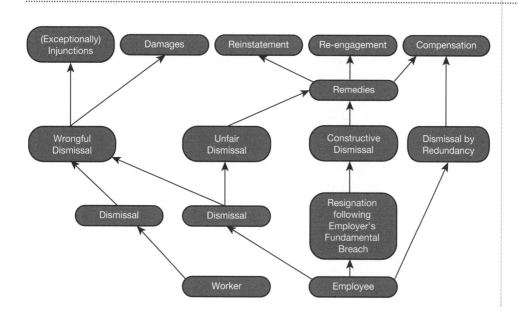

INTRODUCTION

Almost inevitably, an employment relationship will at some time have to come to an end. Perhaps the individual will want to leave their current employment to explore new opportunities, they may be surplus to the requirements of the business, or perhaps the individual will have acted in a way that the employer finds unacceptable and they will be dismissed. This chapter explains the protection afforded to employees against **unfair dismissal** and constructive dismissal; identifies the obligations on employers to fairly dismiss an employee; and contrasts the content of this chapter and Chapter 7 in exploring whether the common law route (**wrongful dismissal**) or the statutory route (unfair dismissal) is the most appropriate following the employer's termination of the employment contract.

Key Definition: Unfair dismissal

A dismissal in breach of statutory requirements – the Employment Rights Act (ERA) 1996. When considering unfair dismissal, always look at ERA 1996 s. 98 in relation to the reasonableness of the employer's decision to dismiss.

Key Definition: Wrongful dismissal

A dismissal in breach of the contract of employment, most commonly seen when an individual is unjustifiably dismissed contrary to the required notice period.

It is important, from the outset, to note the following basic facts:

- wrongful dismissal involves a dismissal of an employee/worker/independent contractor in breach of his/her contract;
- unfair dismissal involves a dismissal contrary to legislation (ERA 1996);
- only individuals with 'employee' employment status have protection from an unfair dismissal.

'Unfair dismissal' offers a greater range of protection than that afforded in wrongful dismissal claims, but the qualification criteria for unfair dismissal are significantly more onerous. A summary of the routes of unfair and wrongful dismissal claims is included in Figure 8.1.

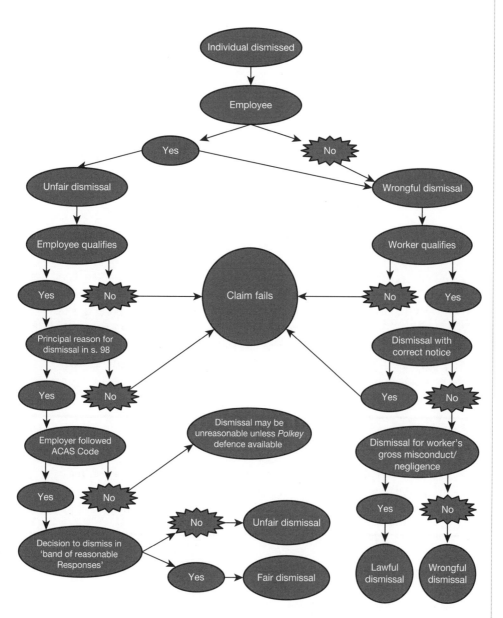

Figure 8.1 Routes to unfair dismissal and wrongful dismissal

SOME BRIEF PRELIMINARY POINTS

Employee status?

A definition of 'employee' is provided in the Employment Rights Act (ERA) 1996 s. 230 but this is deliberately circular and broad. One reason is because employment status is determined on a mix of law and fact – this means the law (ERA 1996 s. 230 and the common law cases) and fact (the facts of each individual case) determines employment status. See Chapter 4 for instruction on determining employment status.

Time limits for claims

Unfair dismissal claims must be lodged at an employment tribunal within three months of the effective date of termination (essentially the last day worked). In *Hawes & Curtis v Arfan & Mirza* [2012] UKEAT/0229/12/JOJ the EAT held that an employment tribunal is entitled to take into account an (unsuccessful) internal appeal against a **summary dismissal** which purports to alter the effective date of termination (EDT). While ERA 1996 s. 97(1) provides that the EDT is determined objectively, the EAT held that a summary dismissal is effective on the date on which the termination of employment took place.

Key Definition: Summary dismissal

A dismissal without notice – perhaps referred to as being 'sacked on the spot'. Essentially, the employer has not conducted any investigation before deciding to dismiss. Such dismissals can be justified (lawful) or unjustified (wrongful).

Required notice periods in termination of the contract

The contract of employment should identify the required notice period to be given by the employer and employee. Where no contractual notice period is identified, ERA 1996 s. 86 provides the information given in Table 7.1 (p. 100).

Note that 12 weeks is the maximum statutory notice period applicable.

These rates are applicable to open-ended contracts. On fixed-term contracts, if no early termination clause (notice period) is included, the innocent party whose contract has been unjustifiably terminated is entitled to the balance of the contract.

Important point to remember: where there has been a summary dismissal of an individual with a fixed-term contract, always consider a claim of wrongful dismissal first – it may provide far more compensation than a claim of unfair dismissal.

Payments in lieu of notice

The issue of notice periods is important because, where no fault exists on either party, the contract of employment may be brought to an end through the issuing of the correct notice. Therefore, a contract of employment may provide, for example, that the employment relationship may be terminated by either party having given one months' notice of their intention to terminate the agreement. The consequence of such an action is that the parties continue with the contract of employment until this notice period has been worked. Quite often employers, having dismissed an individual, will want them to leave the workplace/office immediately and not continue working the remainder of the

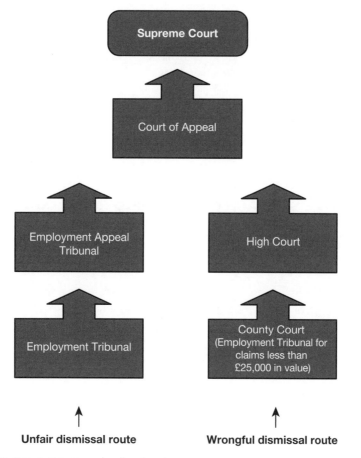

Figure 8.2 Court structure in dismissal cases

contract (the notice period). The employer may wish to pay the worker in advance the wages owed for the notice period. Motivation for such action can arise when the employer does not want the worker to steal corporate information or try to get colleagues to leave the employment and join them in a competing business. This is an appropriate response by an employer, although there is no implied right for the employer to dismiss a worker with a PILON. Such a right has to be (expressly) incorporated into the contract (*Morrish v NLT Group* [2007] CSIH 56).

Where is the claim heard?

Unfair dismissal claims are heard exclusively in employment tribunals with appeals being heard at the EAT. The court structure involving employment disputes is demonstrated in Figure 8.2.

WHAT IS UNFAIR DISMISSAL?

In 1971 legislative measures introduced the right for qualifying employees not to be unfairly dismissed (now ERA 1996 s. 94(1)). Where wrongful dismissal was concerned with adherence to contractual issues, unfair dismissal legislation provided for a broader range of protection – extending this to dismissals that were either substantially and/or procedurally unfair, and imposing the requirement for an employer to demonstrate that he/she had acted 'reasonably' in choosing to dismiss.

AN EMPLOYEE'S BREACH OF THE EMPLOYMENT CONTRACT

While notice periods for the termination of the contract of employment are identified in the contract and/or statute, providing the notice period or PILON is not always necessary.

Situations exist where the actions of an employee would amount to a serious and fundamental breach of the contract (a gross misconduct), which allow the other party (here it is the employer) to accept the breach and terminate the contract. The term used for where an individual's contract of employment is terminated without notice is a 'summary dismissal'. As identified in Chapter 7, at common law this is quite an acceptable course of action. However, caution should be exercised when dealing with employees who have protection under ERA 1996. If for no other reason, the ACAS Code of Practice requires an employer to have conducted a reasonable investigation into a misconduct and possess 'reasonable grounds' upon which to hold belief of (gross) misconduct. Hence, as a general rule, summary dismissals are more likely to be accepted as justifiable in wrongful dismissal actions than they are in claims of unfair dismissal.

DIFFERENCE BETWEEN THE COMMON LAW AND STATUTORY RIGHTS

Insofar as the employer provides the correct notice period (and pay) for the termination of the contract of employment, an individual has no claim for wrongful dismissal. However, even where the notice period is provided, the decision to dismiss may still amount to an unfair dismissal depending on the employer's reason, for example, dismissing an employee because of their race is an automatically unfair reason to dismiss.

QUALIFICATION CRITERIA NECESSARY FOR PROTECTION UNDER UNFAIR DISMISSAL

The following is a list of the criteria necessary for protection under unfair dismissal:

- the individual has 'employee' status;
- they have been continuously employed by the same employer for at least two years prior to the dismissal (unless there is an automatically unfair dismissal);
- the employee demonstrates that they have been dismissed (unfairly); and
- the claim is submitted to the tribunal within three months of the EDT.

Having qualified for protection, the employer may seek to defeat a claim of unfair dismissal where they have a potentially fair reason to dismiss the employee, and they have acted reasonably in choosing to dismiss.

WHAT MAKES AN UNFAIR DISMISSAL 'UNFAIR'?

Employees are granted the right not to be unfairly dismissed by ERA 1996 s. 94. The key issue is 'unfairness' in the choice of dismissal, and there are two elements that could make the dismissal of an employee unfair – a substantive element and/or a procedural element.

Substantive/procedural unfair dismissal

The substantive element

Refers to the substance of the reason for the dismissal – did the employee do something so wrong that the employer was justified in dismissing them? ERA 1996 s. 98 provides a list of what are called 'potentially fair reasons to dismiss'. It is absolutely crucial that you are familiar with these as this will be the starting point for a discussion of fairness.

The employer must select one (or more) of these five potentially fair reasons as the *principal* reason for the decision to dismiss. If the employer fails in this task, the employer's argument that this amounted to a fair dismissal will likely fail at this stage. NOTE: where the employer chooses more than one reason for the dismissal, they must justify each (the tribunal will not identify which of the reasons was the more important). Hence, the employer should exercise caution when selecting the reason for dismissing the employee.

The procedural element

Having selected the reason for the dismissal under the categories listed in ERA 1996 s. 98, the employer must demonstrate that they acted fairly by following the correct disciplinary/dismissal procedure. Remember, s. 98 outlines 'potentially' fair reasons – the employer must still have acted reasonably in the choice of dismissing the employee, having gathered evidence or holding a reasonable belief that the employee had committed some wrong.

The substantive element in more detail

Potentially fair reasons to dismiss

ERA 1996 s. 98 identifies five potentially fair reasons that may justify a dismissal. The employer must explain how the employee's conduct fell into one of these categories:

SOME OTHER SUBSTANTIAL REASON OF A KIND TO JUSTIFY A DISMISSAL (S. 98(1)(B))

This is perhaps the broadest category of potentially fair reasons to dismiss and is usually seen where an employer has re-organised the business – changed working hours or unilaterally altered the contract. In the past, it has enabled dismissals on the basis of an employee's refusal to agree to be bound by a new contract incorporating a restraint of trade clause (*RS Components v Irwin* [1973] IRLR 239) and even provided for the dismissal of an employee whose attitude at work was sufficiently unpleasant to amount to a breach of the implied term of trust and confidence (*Perkin v St George's Healthcare NHS Trust* [2005] EWCA Civ. 1174). The tribunal will not assess the business reason for the employer's re-organisation of their business. The employer knows the business better than the tribunal. The tribunal will ensure that the re-organisation is the 'real' reason for the dismissal and that the employer has followed the appropriate dismissal procedures.

CAPABILITY/QUALIFICATIONS OF THE EMPLOYEE (S. 98(2)(A))

ERA 1996 identifies that capability to perform a job involves skill, aptitude, health or any other physical or mental quality. Hence, an employee engaged to perform some specific role in an organisation should have the ability/skill to do that (insofar as the employer has provided adequate training). An employee may become incapable of performing the job through ill health (but be careful of transgression of the Disability Discrimination Act 1995 / EA 2010 here) or they may be promoted to a new job that they cannot perform. Further, an act of gross incompetence/negligence may be indicative of a breach of capability as in *Alidair v Taylor* [1978] IRLR 82 where a pilot forgot to lower the plane's under-carriage when landing.

THE EMPLOYEE'S CONDUCT (S. 98(2)(B))

Misconduct may involve a series of relatively minor breaches that culminate in a dismissal. The employer must have raised the problem with the employee about their conduct first, and provided them with time to improve before deciding to dismiss for this reason.

A gross misconduct is a one-off serious event that would justify a dismissal (for example stealing, assaults at work, etc.).

KEY CASE ANALYSIS: *British Home Stores v Burchell* [1978] IRLR 379

Background

- An employee of the store was dismissed on suspicion of theft.
- There was a lack of any firm evidence that the employee had committed this misconduct.
- The employer dismissed the employee, this dismissal was held by the tribunal to be unfair, and the case was appealed to the EAT.

Principle established

- The EAT established what became known as the 'Burchell principles'.
- The significance of the case is that employers are not required to hold proof of misconduct to justify a dismissal on that basis. Rather, they are required to hold reasonable grounds upon which to hold the belief.
- Therefore, a list of three steps were established to satisfy the Burchell principles:

  1 The employer must honestly believe the employee is guilty of the offence.
  2 The employer must establish reasonable grounds upon which to hold this belief.
  3 The employer must have carried out as much investigation into the matter as was reasonable in all of the circumstances.

KEY CASE ANALYSIS: *Parr v Whitbread* [1990]

Background

- The claimant had been employed as a manager for the firm and, along with three other employees, was dismissed when a large quantity of money was discovered to have been stolen from the employer's premises.
- Following the employer's investigation into the missing money, it was concluded that a theft had taken place and there was no evidence of a break-in or that any outside body had been responsible for the theft.
- Part of the employer's investigation involved a hearing with each of the four employees. These were the only people who could have been involved in the theft or have any information about it, although each person interviewed failed to admit the offence and failed to provide any information which would assist the employer in the investigation.
- Being unable to identify the thief (if indeed there was just one), the employer dismissed all four employees for gross misconduct.

Principle established

- The EAT heard an appeal on the basis of whether these dismissals were fair.
- The EAT concluded that the dismissals were fair due to the theft – which was correctly identified as gross misconduct. The employer had conducted a reasonable investigation and could not identify the individual(s) responsible.
- As this case involved dismissal of four employees, and presumably there may have been three employees who were innocent of the offence, the EAT established the following guidelines to ensure fairness when an employer wishes to dismiss a group of employees for misconduct:

  1 a dismissal for such an offence must have been justified (such as gross misconduct);
  2 the employer must have conducted a reasonable investigation and followed the correct procedure (such as established by ACAS);
  3 the employer must reasonably believe that the offence could have been committed by more than one person;
  4 the employer must have reasonably identified those individuals who could have committed the offence;
  5 following a reasonable investigation, the employer is unable to identify the culprit.

However, what happens where an employer suspects misconduct, but lacks firm evidence to substantiate the claim? Remember, employment relationships are based on the mutual trust and confidence between the parties. If this is no longer present, there can be no employment relationship. Dismissals on the basis of suspected behaviour may be fair where they follow the 'Burchell principles'.

Therefore, when applying the Burchell principles, an employer is required to have conducted a reasonable investigation. What is reasonable is determined by the nature of the offence, the implications for the employee such as whether they would be disciplined or dismissed, and the size of the organisation and the resources available. Clearly a large organisation may be expected to establish a committee or group from outside the department in which the employee works, to conduct as reasonable and impartial an investigation as possible. For smaller organisations, perhaps those employing one or two people, this simply isn't possible and an investigation held by the employer, and meetings conducted by this employer, may be the only resources available.

An employer may be faced with a situation where there is more than one employee who is potentially responsible for an act of misconduct. What can the employer do in such circumstances when the culprit cannot be identified? The answer was provided by the EAT in *Parr v Whitbread* [1990] IRLR 39:

REDUNDANCY OF THE EMPLOYEE (S. 98(2)(C))

Redundancy is a potentially fair reason to dismiss as the employer is closing the business or reducing the workforce due to an economic, technical or organisational reason (although often the employee will be entitled to compensation – a redundancy payment). It may be assumed that the employer would not make these dismissals unless it was economically necessary. Hence it is deemed potentially fair as the employer either has no work for the employee to perform, or the employer has to reduce the workforce to reduce costs. Dismissal by reason of redundancy may be unfair where the employee was unfairly selected (for example, against an agreed procedure) or if the selection was made due to the employee's affiliation with a trade union.

TO ENGAGE THE EMPLOYEE WOULD BE TO CONTRAVENE A STATUTE (S. 98(2)(D))

A most common example of this section at work is where an employee who is required to drive as part of their job is banned from driving. The employee has acted in such a way that they cannot carry out their function at work and as such may be fairly dismissed.

On-the-spot question

Does an employer require actual proof of an employee's wrongdoing before deciding to dismiss? What is the level of proof required to satisfy the tribunal that the employer's actions were reasonable?

The procedural element in more detail

An employer must demonstrate that the decision to dismiss was fair (satisfied in the substantive test) and reasonable (by following the correct procedure). The fairness of the decision will depend on the information that the employer held *at the time of choosing to dismiss* (*Polkey v AE Dayton Services* [1987] IRLR 503). Hence, the employer must have carried out a reasonable investigation into the incident that has led to their decision to consider a dismissal.

Reasonableness is established on the basis of both the ACAS Code of Practice (1): Discipline and Grievance, and the information held by the employer. In *Anglian Homes Ltd v Kelly* [2004] IRLR 793 the Court of Appeal instructed tribunals not to substitute its own decision on whether an employee's action would have led it to dismiss, for the decision taken by the employer. The tribunal should determine whether the employer's decision fell into the 'band of reasonable responses' as established in *Iceland Frozen Foods Ltd v Jones* [1982] IRLR 439. Essentially, the question the tribunal should ask is: 'Could another reasonable employer have acted in the same way in choosing to dismiss the employee in the case before the tribunal?' If yes, this dismissal will have fallen into the band of reasonable responses and be fair. If no, then it was a disproportionately harsh decision and the dismissal will be unfair. Further, in *Nejjary v Aramark Ltd* [2012] UKEAT/0054/12/CEA the EAT held that an employment tribunal is only entitled to take into account matters which the employer raised as the reason for the dismissal. Here the tribunal erred in taking into account matters that the employer had not when deciding whether the choice to dismiss fell into the band of reasonable responses.

The tribunal looks at the investigation carried out by the employer into the matter that led to the dismissal, considers whether the employer followed the correct procedures before making the decision, identifies if the decision to dismiss falls into the band of reasonable responses, and finally considers whether another reasonable employer could have drawn the same conclusions and dismissed the employee (for an example of how to conduct an unreasonable investigation see *Stuart v London City Airport* [2012] UKEAT/0273/12).

The ACAS Code of Practice (1): Discipline and Grievance

The Code is not 'law' as it was intended to be flexible and not overly prescriptive. However, tribunals will expect employers to have followed the main elements of the Code which require that:

- Disciplinary/dismissal matters should be raised in a timely fashion and dealt with promptly by both parties.
- The employer should act consistently in relation to the matter leading to the disciplinary/dismissal action.
- Employers are required to have conducted a reasonable investigation into the matter to establish the facts.
- Employers should hold a meeting where any allegations may be put to the employee, and allow the employee to respond.
- Employers should take action (where appropriate) to substantiate any information put forward by the employee at the meeting.
- Employers should ensure the employee is aware of their right to be accompanied at the meeting (by a colleague or trades union official).
- Following the fulfillment of these procedures, the employer should then consider all possible responses before a decision to dismiss is made (taking into account factors such as the employment/disciplinary history of the employee).
- Employers should allow the employee the option of an appeal of any formal decision.

The Code establishes a model for fairness and transparency that should ensure a decision to dismiss/discipline an employee is reasonable. Where an employer unreasonably fails to follow the Code, or where the employee fails to participate in hearings, etc., tribunals have the power to adjust (raise/lower as appropriate) any award of compensation by up to 25 per cent.

Be aware that disciplining an employee who has been through a disciplinary procedure is usually the conclusion of that matter. However, there is no so-called 'double-jeopardy' rule in employment law and an employer may be able to put the employee through a second disciplinary procedure where this is deemed appropriate. In *Christou & Ward v Haringey* [2012] UKEAT/0298/11/DM, an infamous case in England involving errors in social services which contributed to the death of a baby, the social workers involved in the case had been through the Authority's 'Simplified Disciplinary Procedure' and issued with a written warning (the maximum penalty available). However, following media interest in the incident and dismissals of senior staff, the social workers were subject to a second disciplinary procedure where they were dismissed. The EAT held (on a majority) that the dismissals were not unfair, although this was an unusual case and most cases of disciplinary action would not involve two sets of disciplinary procedures on the same facts.

...r discovered reasons

An 'after discovered reason' is the term used where an employer, having already dismissed an individual, later discovers a reason/proof of misconduct that would have justified the individual's dismissal.

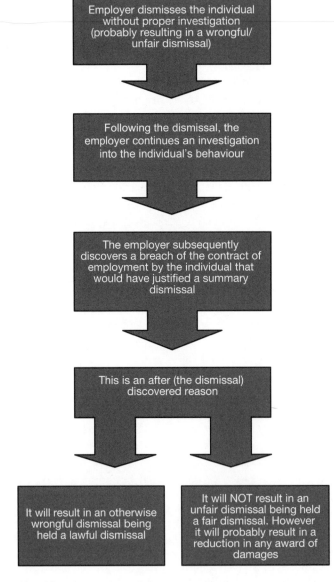

Figure 8.3 Effect of after discovered reasons following dismissal

The distinction between wrongful dismissal and unfair dismissal is again demonstrated here:

- An after discovered reason justifying a summary dismissal is permissible in evidence in claims of wrongful dismissal, i.e. it would make an otherwise wrongful dismissal a lawful dismissal.
- An after discovered reason will not make an unfair dismissal a fair dismissal. This is because the fairness of the reason for the dismissal is determined on the basis of the evidence held by the employer at the time of the decision to dismiss. However, it will lead to a reduction in any award of compensatory damages and it will prevent the award of reinstatement or re-engagement. Hence, even after a hasty dismissal, it is wise for an employer to continue an investigation to substantiate, with as much proof as is available, evidence of misconduct by the individual that would have warranted a dismissal (see Figure 8.3).

AUTOMATICALLY UNFAIR REASONS TO DISMISS

Part of the qualifying criteria to claim unfair dismissal is that the employee must have completed a minimum of two years' continuous service. However, various statutes provide protection against dismissal for reasons that are deemed automatically unfair. The nature of 'automatically' unfair reasons to dismiss is that the protection is afforded immediately – there is no requirement for the two years' continuous service to have been completed.

The following is a (non-exhaustive) list of examples of dismissals that would be considered automatically unfair:

- dismissals due to a spent conviction under the Rehabilitation of Offenders Act 1974;
- dismissals due to trade union membership/activities (s. 238A(2) Trade Union and Labour Relations (Consolidation) Act 1992);
- dismissals due to the pregnancy of the individual or any related illness (s. 99 ERA 1996);
- dismissal because the employee took steps to avert danger to health and safety at work (s. 100 ERA 1996);
- dismissals where the employee has made a protected public interest disclosure (s. 103A of ERA 1996), as provided through the Public Interest Disclosure Act 1998;
- dismissal in connection with the employee asserting a statutory right (s. 104 ERA 1996);
- dismissal through an unfair selection for redundancy (s. 105 ERA 1996);
- dismissal on the transfer of an undertaking (reg. 7 TUPE Regulations 2006).

WHICH CLAIM? UNFAIR OR WRONGFUL DISMISSAL?

Having considered in Chapter 7 wrongful dismissal, and having now almost completed discussion of unfair dismissal, it may be wise to consider which route would be the most appropriate for a dismissed individual to take. In this respect, consider the following issues when making your decision:

- Only individuals with 'employee' status qualify for unfair dismissal. Individuals without this status must bring the claim for wrongful dismissal.
- The remedies in each claim are different. Unfair dismissal may enable the successful claimant to an award of re-instatement (the primary remedy) or re-engagement, and compensation. The remedy available in wrongful dismissal is limited to compensation (although exceptionally an injunction may be awarded to prevent a dismissal – *Irani v South West Hampshire Health Authority* [1985]).
- The level of compensation available following a successful claim of unfair dismissal is limited to £68,400 for the compensatory award (updated bi-annually). There is no ceiling to the damages that may be awarded in wrongful dismissal.
- There is no legal aid available in the presentation of an unfair dismissal claim (although it does exist for discrimination matters), but it may be available in wrongful dismissal (for discussion see *Wright v Michael Wright Supplies Ltd & Anor* [2013] EWCA Civ. 234).
- The areas of protection – dismissals due to discrimination; membership of/activities in trade unions etc. – are broader in unfair dismissal than in wrongful dismissal.
- 'After discovered reasons' will not make an otherwise unfair dismissal, fair; but they are available to make an otherwise wrongful dismissal lawful.
- The level of compensation in unfair dismissal claims is (largely) fixed on the basis of a calculation outlined in ERA 1996. This is based, in part, on the employee's number of continuous years in the employment. Where the employment is of a fixed duration (a fixed-term contract) and there is no contractual early termination clause, damages in wrongful dismissal may be awarded for the balance of the contract NOT the notice period applicable (as would have been the case in an open-ended contract). Therefore this could potentially lead to substantially greater damages being awarded (the average compensation awarded in unfair dismissal claims in 2009–10 was just £9,120).

On-the-spot question

? The government removed almost all access to legal aid in employment law from 1 April 2013 to reduce costs. How have the cost savings improved the provision of justice through employment tribunals where the parties are unrepresented, and what are the case management problems faced by the employment judge in such circumstances?

CONSTRUCTIVE DISMISSAL

Constructive dismissal is not, as such, a third route to pursue for an individual whose contract of employment has been terminated. Rather, constructive dismissal was established in relation to unfair dismissal, as one of the qualification criteria for that remedy is for the individual to demonstrate that they had been dismissed. It is not difficult to imagine a scenario whereby an employer may have fundamentally changed or varied a contract to which the employee did not agree. The employee's only option would be to resign. If the employer had not dismissed the employee, there would evidently have been no claim of unfair dismissal permissible.

To protect the employee against such a consequence, the law provided for access to unfair dismissal, via constructive dismissal, where an employer had fundamentally breached the employee's contract of employment. Therefore, while the employee had not been dismissed, they could choose to accept the employer's action as a fundamental breach (repudiation) and pursue a claim of unfair dismissal (ss. 95(1)(c) and 136(1)(c)).

Examples of fundamental breaches that have enabled successful constructive unfair dismissal claims include:

- the harassment and bullying of an individual (*Reed v Stedman* [1999] IRLR 299);
- a unilateral reduction in an employee's pay (*Industrial Rubber Products v Gillon* [1977] IRLR 389); and
- an unreasonable accusation of theft (*Robinson v Crompton Parkinson* [1978] IRLR 61).

However, actions by an immediate manager may not amount to a fundamental breach of trust and confidence where senior managers took steps to rectify the situation (in *Assamoi v Spirit Pub Company (Services) Ltd* [2012] UKEAT/0050/11). This does not affect the current law established in *Bournemouth University Higher Education Corporation v Buckland* [2010] ICR 908 CA where subsequent action cannot cure a breach that has already taken place.

It is important to note that an employer's fundamental breach of the contract does not have to be the principal reason for the employee's claim of constructive dismissal. Insofar as the employee resigns due, in part, to the employer's fundamental breach, this will satisfy the requirement of being the reason for the dismissal (see *Logan v Celyn House Ltd* [2012] UKEAT/0069/12/JOJ).

These fundamental breaches may enable the employee to bring a claim of unfair dismissal where they act quickly and make an outward sign of not accepting the change. Where the employee remains silent and works under new conditions – such as the unilateral reduction in pay imposed by the employer in *Gillon* [1977] – it may be held as evidence of the employee's affirmation of the change and they will lose the right to claim (*Holland v Glendale Industries Ltd* [1998] ICR 493).

One tactic that the employee can use in such circumstances is to work 'under protest'. The individual maintains the current employment (albeit under the new terms/changes imposed by the employer), but preserves the right to bring a claim for the breach at a later date – such as when they have secured another job (see Figure 8.4).

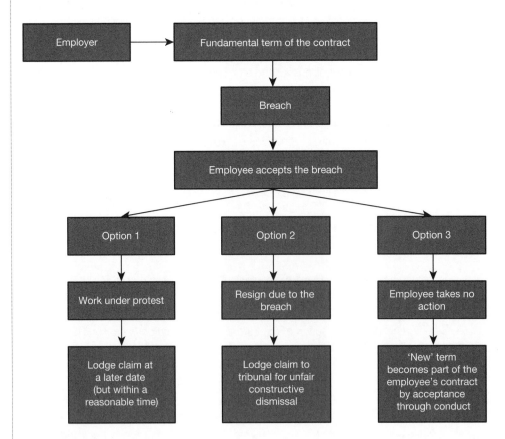

Figure 8.4 Options for an employee following an employer's fundamental breach

The rules for establishing a constructive dismissal claim were identified by the Court of Appeal in *Western Excavating v Sharp* [1978] IRLR 27 and can be distilled into a three-stage test:

1. the employer must have breached an express or implied term, or clearly identified that they would no longer be bound by the contract;
2. the breach must have been fundamental/essential to the contract; and
3. the employee must have accepted the breach and informed the employer of this within a reasonable time.

On-the-spot question

 An employer has discovered stock-irregularities and identified only three employees that had access to the stockroom where the missing goods were kept. What action is available to the employer in light of this problem?

REMEDIES FOR UNFAIR DISMISSAL

Remedies in unfair dismissal are different from those available in wrongful dismissal:

*   re-instatement;
*   re-engagement;
*   compensation (basic award; compensatory award; additional award).

Re-instatement

The primary remedy following a finding of unfair dismissal is re-instatement (although relatively few orders of reinstatement are requested and/or complied with). This is an order of the tribunal that requires the employer to give the unfairly dismissed employee their job back. Where an employer unreasonably refuses to comply with the order, the employer is not forced to re-employ the employee; rather the level of compensation awarded to the employee (damages) is increased.

Re-engagement

Where the employee has been dismissed, the position of employment they occupied may have been filled by the time the case of unfair dismissal is heard at the tribunal (it will be several weeks/months before a case is heard by the tribunal). As such, a tribunal will not order the dismissed employee to be re-hired to the same job if it no longer exists. The remedy of re-engagement is an option for the tribunal to award in such circumstances. This requires that the offer of alternative employment be made as close to the level of seniority, pay and promotion opportunities as was previously enjoyed.

Compensation

Remedies in unfair dismissal also include compensation. This is a damages payment intended to compensate the employee's direct losses attributable to the dismissal. There are two elements – a basic award, and a compensatory award. Further, where an employee has requested re-instatement or re-engagement and the employer has unreasonably refused to comply, an additional award may be made.

CONCLUSION

This chapter has considered unfair dismissal and constructive dismissal, and provided a brief comparison of these rights with the common law protection against a wrongful dismissal. Chapter 9 addresses the other major form of dismissal – redundancy, and it also identifies the protections for employees when the business in which they are employed is transferred to a new owner. The Transfer of Undertakings Regulations is a significant aspect of employment law and, as seen above, both the transfer of undertakings and redundancy can form an unfair reason to dismiss where done so incorrectly.

FURTHER READING

www.acas.org.uk
ACAS provides practical information for employers and individuals on rights/obligations at work.

Brodie, D. (2002) 'Fair Dealing and the Dismissal Process', *Industrial Law Journal*, Vol. 31, No. 3, p. 294.
A comparative paper considering the application and scope of mutual trust and confidence to the regulation of termination in employment law.

Brodtkorb, T. (2010) 'Employee Misconduct and UK Unfair Dismissal Law: Does the Range of Reasonable Responses Test Require Reform?', *International Journal of Law and Management*, Vol. 52, No. 6, p. 429.
An interesting article critiquing the range of reasonable responses test in unfair dismissal, and offering suggestions for alternative approaches.

Earnshaw, J., Marchington, M., Goodman, J. (2000) 'Unfair to Whom? Discipline and Dismissal in
    Small Establishments', *Industrial Relations Journal*, Vol. 31, No. 1, p. 62.
An article reviewing alternative approaches to workplace disciplinary grievance procedures and
the treatment received by employers in employment tribunals.

Ford, M. (1998) 'Rethinking the Notice Rule', *Industrial Law Journal*, Vol. 27, No. 3, p. 220.
A commentary on the employer's discretion to terminate the contract of employment and limit
damages payments to the duration of the notice period. This encompasses a discussion of
general contractual principles applied to employment relations, and how this is affected by the
power relations between the parties.

Chapter 9
Redundancy and the transfer of undertakings

LEARNING OBJECTIVES

After reading this chapter you should be able to:

- identify the qualifications required of an individual to qualify for protection in redundancy situations and when a business is transferred;
- explain the two broad scenarios that amount to redundancy;
- identify an employer's duty to consult with the workforce/representatives or trade union in the event of redundancies or business transfers;
- explain workers' rights protected through the Transfer of Undertakings (Protection of Employment) (TUPE) Regulations 2006 in the event of a business being sold;
- assess the extent of an employer's ability to justify, as fair, redundancy dismissals where such dismissals are due to an economic, technical or organisational reason.

MIND MAP

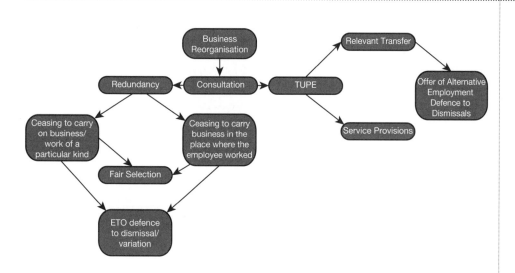

INTRODUCTION

A business may decide to dismiss individuals because of their conduct, abilities or qualifications, or because to continue employing them would be to break the law (see Chapter 8 on unfair dismissal). A business may decide to dismiss individuals because of the sale of a business or its re-organisation. Whether such dismissals are fair is determined in relation to the laws on **redundancy** and transfer of undertakings. A potentially fair reason to dismiss an employee is for redundancy. This occurs in one of two broad scenarios: (1) The employer is ceasing to operate the business (the employer is closing the business down) and all individuals are being dismissed as there is no job for them to perform; and (2) The employer is ceasing to operate a part of the business (due to a re-organisation, for example) and an individual or group of individuals are surplus to the requirements of the business (the work of a particular kind undertaken by the individual(s) has ceased or diminished).

Key Definition: Redundancy

Redundancy occurs when employment at the place of business has ceased; or the work of a particular kind undertaken by the individual(s), at the place where the employee was so employed, has ceased or diminished.

Many employment rights, and the compensation awarded in cases of unfair dismissal and redundancy are based on the number of continuous years of service the employee has amassed. Further, terms and conditions of work identify the rights and responsibilities of employees. Prior to the EU's legislation on the matter – beginning with the Acquired Rights Directive 77/187, and subsequent domestic law of the TUPE Regulations 1981 (SI 1981/1794), a new employer could (and often would) dismiss the existing employees immediately following a transfer, even where the previous employer was selling the business as a going concern. These individuals would have limited compensation (as they had no 'continuous employment' with the new employer) but it became commonplace for those individuals who were dismissed to be offered their 'former' job back by the new employer, albeit on substantially worse terms (lower pay, fewer paid holidays, etc.). TUPE 1981 restricted this power and compelled the new employer (known as the transferee) to honour the terms and conditions of employees, and dismissals associated with the transfer were held as **automatically unfair** – allowing affected employees to seek compensation.

Key Definition: Automatically unfair (reasons to dismiss)

The Employment Rights Act 1996 identifies certain reasons selected by an employer for dismissal as automatically unfair. Dismissal on the basis of a transfer of an undertaking, where the employer does not have an economic, technical or organisational reason defence, will be held automatically unfair.

REDUNDANCY

This topic is particularly relevant in the current economic climate. Where a business is in financial difficulties and may need to reorganise (such as by closing parts of the organisation that are not/less profitable than others), the result may be that some employees need to be dismissed as they are surplus to requirements/a downturn in business diminishes the need for the work undertaken by the employee, or indeed all of the employees may be dismissed as the entire business is closed down (such as through insolvency). This may result in the redundancy of the employees, and employees dismissed for redundancy are entitled to a minimum statutory redundancy payment.

Qualifications to claim

Employers may have to make redundancy payments to individuals where the individual satisfies the following criteria (as identified in ss. 135–165 ERA 1996):

- they possess 'employee' status;
- they have been continuously employed by the same employer for at least two years before the date of redundancy;
- they have been dismissed (and for the reason of redundancy); and
- they are not in one of the excluded categories of employee.

The employer will identify that the principal reason for the dismissal of the employee is redundancy (see *Fish v Glen Golf Club* [2012] UKEATS/0057/11/BI). The tribunal may seek to satisfy itself that this is indeed the principal reason for the dismissal, but it is not entitled to critique the rationale or necessity of the employer's decision to make redundancies/close the business (*Moon v Homeworthy Furniture* [1976] IRLR 298).

The key issue from the above qualifying criteria is what constitutes a dismissal, although note that s. 163(2) presumes redundancy is the reason for the dismissal and places the burden on the employer to disprove this. 'Effective' dismissal requires that the employer has given the employee a specific date on which their employment will end (this is known as being put under notice of dismissal) rather than an employer's future intention of redundancy (*Morton Sundour Fabrics v Shaw* [1966] CLY 4472). Hence an actual dismissal; the non-renewal of a fixed-term contract or conduct by the employer entitling the employee to terminate the contract will amount, in this regard, to dismissal by redundancy (s. 136).

Redundancy and 'work of a particular kind'

For the purposes of ERA 1996, an employee who is dismissed shall be taken to be dismissed by reason of redundancy if the dismissal is attributable wholly or mainly to:

(a) the fact that their employer has ceased, or intends to cease:
   (i)   to carry on the business for the purposes of which the employee was employed; or
   (ii) to carry on that business in the place where the employee was so employed; or
(b) the fact that the requirements of that business have ceased or diminished or are expected to cease or diminish in regard to:
   (i)   employees carrying out work of a particular kind; or
   (ii) employees carrying out work of a particular kind in the place where the employee was so employed by the employer. (Note that a diminution in work does not necessarily need to involve a reduction in the numbers of employees employed – see *Packman v Fauchon* [2012] UKEAT/0017/12/LA).

'Place where the employee was so employed'

An employer may decide that running the business from a particular place of employment is either going to cease or will require fewer employees. Where the employer has businesses in other places (for example, in other regions of the country) the affected employees may be offered re-deployment at this alternative location. Some employees may accept the re-deployment, and for others it may not be suitable.

The problem arose where employers were increasingly using mobility clauses in contracts of employment. Such a clause (which must be used reasonably) enabled the employer to require the employee to work at an alternative place of employment insofar as this was in accordance with the mobility clause. Such clauses are increasingly important to employers as they allow them to move expert employees to businesses where their skills are most needed. Where such a clause existed, the employer, having ceased trading from a particular place of employment, or required fewer employees, could utilise the mobility clause requiring employees to redeploy elsewhere. Those who accepted the offer worked in the new place of employment (they were redeployed), those who refused were not made redundant for the purposes of the law (as the 'place of employment' criterion was not satisfied in accordance with the legislation). That position changed in the following case.

KEY CASE ANALYSIS: *Bass Leisure Ltd v Thomas* **[1994] IRLR 104**

Background

- Thomas, based in Coventry, was employed to collect money from fruit machines in that area.
- The employer decided to close the business in Coventry and, invoking a mobility clause, required Thomas to redeploy to a workplace 20 miles away.
- The contract required the employer to take into account the employee's personal and domestic circumstances before enforcing the term. The employer failed to do so.
- Thomas refused, resigned, and claimed **constructive dismissal** on the basis of redundancy.

Principle established

- The Employment Appeal Tribunal (EAT) held that the 'place' where an employee was employed for redundancy payment purposes is to be established by a factual inquiry, taking into account the employee's fixed or changing places of work.
- Any contractual terms which identify the place of employment and its extent (e.g. mobility clauses) are to be taken into account, but they are not terms which provide for the employee to be transferred. (The test was approved by the Court of Appeal in *High Table Ltd v Horst* [1997] IRLR 513).

Where a mobility clause exists, and the employee regularly works in various locations, cessation of trading at a particular location may not be evidence of redundancy where the employee continues to work in other locations. That specific location may not be the 'place of employment' for the purposes of ERA 1996 (as demonstrated in *Horst* [1997]).

BUSINESS RE-ORGANISATIONS

Employers will often re-organise a business to improve its fortunes. This may involve dismissals, but can also include variations to employees' contracts of employment – hours of work, methods of working (technological changes), etc. Where the job function remains the same, yet there has been a substantial alteration in the terms and conditions of the contract, there is no redundancy (*North Riding Garages v Butterwick* [1967] 2 QB 56). The question the tribunal will ask is whether the job itself has changed (indicative of redundancy) or whether it is merely the way of doing the job which has changed (this is a question of adaptability).

Most business re-organisations will amount to a dismissal where the employee refuses to accept the change to the employment (where the employee resigns due to the change and claims constructive unfair dismissal). However, this will most likely be a fair dismissal under s. 98(1)(b) ERA 1996 for 'some other substantial reason'.

Key Definition: Constructive dismissal

Where an employer radically or fundamentally changes the contract to the employee's detriment (such as altering terms and conditions and this is associated with the transfer of a business), the employee is entitled to treat this unilateral change as a repudiation, resign, and claim constructive dismissal.

Selection for redundancy

Where a business is to cease operation and close, with all employees being dismissed, there is no choice in who will be redundant and hence a selection policy is not needed. Where only part(s) of the business are to be reduced and some employees will be retained while others will face redundancy, it is essential that a fair selection procedure is used. This will not only avoid claims of discrimination and unfairness by those who were selected (with the resultant additional claims for unfair dismissal at tribunal) but it will also assist in maintaining good industrial relations.

At its essence, a fair procedure will involve the employer communicating and consulting with the employees directly, a trade union or the employees' representatives (at the very least in accordance with the statute) at an early a stage as possible. This will provide information and warning about possible redundancies, and allow those interested parties to make representations to the employer prior to any final decisions being made. Further, the employer should seek to identify any alternative employment opportunities in the workplace (in different divisions of the organisation, for example) or alternative employment opportunities (at different sites, etc.) for the affected employees to minimise, as far as is possible, the negative effects of the redundancies.

On-the-spot question

 What features would establish a fair selection policy? Explain with whom an employer should consult to ensure fairness and identify the legal and business consequences when this is not undertaken.

In *Williams v Compair Maxam* [1982] ICR 156, the EAT set out five principles of good industrial relations practice that should generally be followed when employees are represented by a recognised trade union:

1   to give as much warning as possible;
2   to consult with the union, particularly relating to the criteria to be applied in selection for redundancy;
3   to adopt objective rather than subjective criteria for selection, for example, experience, length of service, attendance, etc.;
4   to select in accordance with the criteria, considering any representations made by the union regarding selection; and
5   to consider the possibility of re-deployment rather than dismissal.

In relation to (3) above, the EAT held in *Mitchells of Lancaster (Brewers) Ltd v Tattersall* [2012] UKEAT/0605/11/SM showed that some use of subjective criteria was reasonable. The EAT considered that 'the concept of a criterion only being valid if it can be "scored or assessed" causes us a little concern, as it could be invoked to limit selection procedures to box-ticking exercises' (para. 21).

Situations where a dismissal is deemed not to occur

The following is a list of situations where an employee faced with redundancy, will not be deemed to have been dismissed:

- where a suitable offer of renewal or re-engagement is made with the same employer;
- where an offer of suitable employment is made by associated companies;
- where there is a 'relevant transfer' of an undertaking (TUPE 2006 applies here);
- where an employee leaves prematurely before being subject to a redundancy notice (*Morton Sundour Fabrics Ltd v Shaw* [1966]).

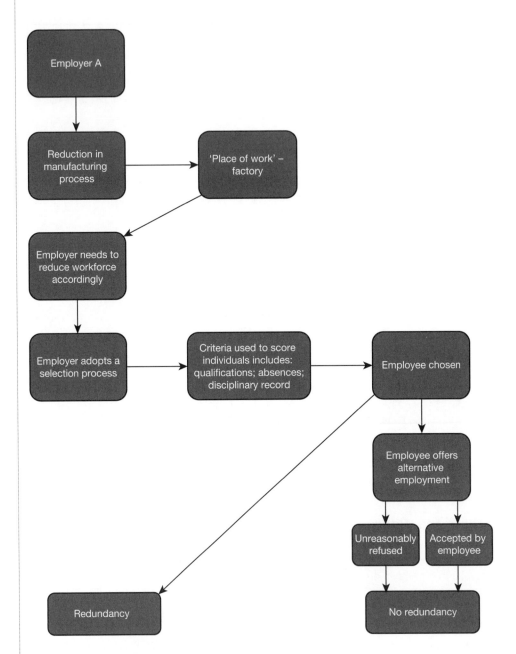

Figure 9.1 Example of redundancy

Offers of alternative employment

Making an employee redundant results in a dismissal, however, where the employer offers the employee suitable alternative employment or re-deployment with the employer or an associated employer, there may be no dismissal. The employee may be expected to consider such an offer as they have up to four weeks to trial the employment and decide if they find it suitable. If in this time the employee does not find the employment suitable, this will not prevent them seeking a redundancy payment (s. 138).

Unreasonable refusal of suitable alternative employment

Where an employer has offered suitable alternative employment to the employee, and the employee unreasonably refuses such an offer, the employee will lose the right to claim a redundancy payment. This is subject to (1) the offer being suitable (assessed objectively); and (2) assessment of the employee's acceptance or refusal (assessed with regard to the particular employee). In the first example, the offer of a job in a 'floating pool' of teachers was not a suitable one for a head teacher because it reduced the status of the job: *Taylor v Kent CC* [1969] 2 QB 560. With regards to the second issue, re-deployment from Mayfair, London, to an office above a sex shop in Soho was unreasonably refused by a female employee in *Fuller v Stephanie Bowman Ltd* [1977] IRLR 87 (see Figure 9.1. for an example of redundancy).

Redundancy payments

The remedy awarded in cases of redundancy is compensation (although unfair selection or breach of the consultation requirements may result in an unfair dismissal claim and awards of re-instatement and re-engagement). Redundancy payments are calculated in the same way as for unfair dismissal, although years in employment below the age of 18 years are not included in the calculation.

THE TRANSFER OF UNDERTAKINGS (PROTECTION OF EMPLOYMENT) REGULATIONS

Since 1977, the European Union has legislated for the protection of employees' rights at work following the transfer of a business (in legal terms this is called an undertaking). This was achieved through the Council Directive on Acquired Rights (Council Directive 77/187 of 14 February 1977) (updated and replaced in 2001). This, in turn, led to the United Kingdom establishing the Transfer of Undertakings (Protection of Employment) Regulations 1981 (updated in 2006 – SI 2006/246) (TUPE). The Regulations require, very simply, that qualifying employees have their terms and conditions of employment protected when the owner of a business (the transferor) sells the business to the buyer (transferee). This also includes trade union recognition (although the new owner may see fit to derecognise the trade union) and collective bargaining agreements between the former owner and the trade union. A simple example of the operation of the TUPE regulations is where an individual is employed in a high street music retail store. There is an agreement between the owner of the store to sell the business to a buyer. The buyer may require, as part of the deal, that they do not wish to employ any of the existing staff and, therefore, the seller must dismiss all of them before the sale takes place. A dismissal of an individual in such circumstances has nothing to do with their abilities or competence, but rather it may simply be a cost cutting exercise by this 'new' owner (who may seek to hire the same staff on worse terms or employ cheaper labour). This clearly is an unfair situation to individuals employed, and in such circumstances, TUPE protects individuals by making a decision to dismiss on this basis as automatically unfair. The individual will succeed in a claim for unfair dismissal – hence the other requirement, of 'employee' status, is required (see Figure 9.2 for an example of a transfer of an undertaking).

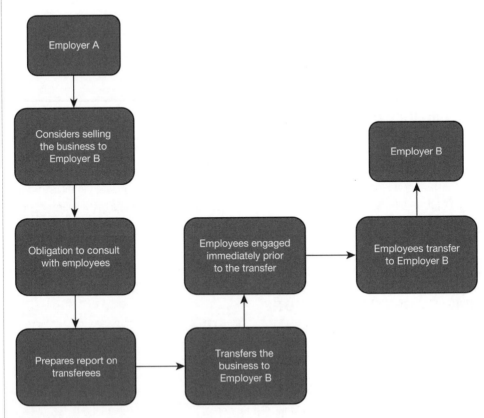

Figure 9.2 Example of transfer of an undertaking

The effects of TUPE are that employees of the business continue to perform their existing role for the new owner. All qualifying existing employees automatically become employees of the new owner, under the same terms and conditions as previously enjoyed, and TUPE applies to all businesses (there is no reduction in responsibility or liability for small businesses). It is also important to recognise that not only does TUPE apply to the transfer of a business, it also applies to the transfer of a service. For example, taking over contractual responsibilities as in *ECM v Cox* [1999] IRLR 559. Attempts to vary the contract against the interests of employees are not allowed (*Foreningen af Arbejdsledere i Danmark v Daddy's Dance Hall A/S* [1988] IRLR 315), even if agreed to by the employee (because employees are protected by statute and they may be coerced/pressured into agreeing to new terms), but variations in the interest of the employee are allowed (*Power v Regent Security Services Ltd* [2007] IRLR 226).

Despite the protections afforded to the individual when the business is transferred, an employee cannot be compelled to transfer to work for the new owner against their will. The result of this action is that there is no dismissal and hence an employee who refuses to transfer will not be able to obtain redundancy/unfair dismissal compensation (*Katsikas v Konstantinidis* [1993] IRLR 179). However, this situation is different to that where an individual refuses to transfer on the belief that they may suffer a detriment under the new owner (such as inferior terms and conditions). This will enable the employee to resign and claim constructive dismissal (*University of Oxford v Humphreys* [2000] IRLR 183).

RESPONSIBILITIES TO EMPLOYEES ON TRANSFER OF A BUSINESS

Owners may have many reasons for choosing to sell a business as a going concern. Some may wish to retire and realise the value of the business; some may choose to sell the business to start an alternative business; others may become ill or their personal circumstances change and this necessitates the sale. In each of these examples (although of course there are many more that could have been given), the sale is of a successful business. It is, by necessity, a commercial reality that many owners choose to sell a business because it is failing. It is also the case that the buyer will want to make changes to that failing business to improve its fortunes. A typical way to achieve this has been through the termination of employees' contracts of employment, or a reduction in the overheads through changes to employees' terms and conditions.

Regulation 7 of TUPE 2006 provides that a dismissal of an employee shall be held as an unfair dismissal if the transfer (or a reason connected with it) is the reason (or principal reason) for the dismissal. The connection to the transfer does not necessarily mean that the dismissal should occur immediately following the transfer. Indeed, in *Taylor v Connex South Eastern Ltd* [2000] UKEAT/12432/99, the fact that the dismissal did not take place until two years after the transfer did not break the 'chain of causation'. Further, simply because other employees are being made redundant/terms of existing employees are being harmonised along with those 'transferred' employees, this does not stop the dismissal or change being connected with the transfer and being for an Economic, Technical or Organisational (ETO) reason (see *Manchester College v Hazel* [2012] UKEAT/0642/11/RN).

This is where TUPE 2006 protects employees who would be otherwise vulnerable to the buyer choosing to dismiss them for no fault, or unilaterally altering the terms and conditions under which they were previously employed. Therefore, employees' rights and terms and conditions of employment are protected on the transfer of the business to a new employer. This means that employees will continue to enjoy those same rights and the incoming employer does not have the legal right to change these (*Credit Suisse v Lister* [1998] EWCA Civ. 1551).

What constitutes a 'transfer'

It is important to recognise that not every business transfer will qualify for TUPE protection. Clearly, there are businesses that simply sell assets such as technology, furniture and so on, the sale of which would not invoke protection of employees rights. The sale of shares will also not qualify (*Brookes and Others v Borough Care Services* [1998] IRLR 636) insofar as the two businesses are run as separate entities (*Millam v The Print Factory (London) 1991 Ltd* [2007] IRLR 526).

On-the-spot question

? Could the sale of shares provide a loophole through which the parent company may simply make employees redundant and avoid TUPE protection? Consider the protection available through the courts in determining whether a transfer falls under TUPE protection.

Relevant transfer

What is required for protection is a 'relevant transfer' and this is identified under Regulation 3 TUPE 2006. This requires that there has been a transfer of an economic entity which retains its identity, or more simply put, the sale of the business as a going concern. It is also important to recognise that not all of a particular business has to be transferred for TUPE to be invoked. For example, businesses, particularly those in the public sector, have often outsourced some aspect of their responsibilities – typically these have been in the cleaning and catering divisions. These would still qualify as a relevant transfer because of the 'economic entity' element of Regulation 3. Where there has been a temporary transfer, as may be applicable in the outsourcing of catering requirements in a public sector organisation, the affected employees will revert back to the employment of that public sector organisation at the cessation of the contract. Where the same contract is then provided to another contractor, these employees will then become the responsibility of the transferee on the same basis as occurred in the first transfer (*Dines and others v (1) Initial Health Care Services Ltd (2) Pall Mall Services Group Ltd* [1995] ICR 11).

Employed 'immediately prior'

If there has been a dismissal before the transfer then TUPE does not protect the employee (*Wilson v St Helens BC* [1998] IRLR 706). Individuals employed immediately prior to the transfer, or who would have been employed had not they being dismissed immediately before the transfer, will automatically become employees of the new owner (Reg 4(3)). This prevents the owner of a business from dismissing employees to facilitate the transfer of the business. In *Litster v Forth Dry Dock and Engineering Co. Ltd* [1989] ICR 341, the House of Lords held that employees dismissed one hour before the transfer of the business were, in accordance with the legislation, deemed as employed 'immediately prior' to the transfer. This was in part due to the collusion between the transferor and the transferee. However, in *Secretary of State for Employment v Spence* [1986] ICR 651, the dismissal of employees, even though the business was sold later that same day, was not held to be immediately prior to the transfer because the receiver in charge of the company sought to protect the interests of creditors through the dismissals, and there was doubt as to whether the sale would be completed.

Service provision

At the time of writing, a transfer of a service provision may amount to a TUPE (Regulation 3). Service provisions are protected by the domestic law (TUPE) but are not a requirement of the parent EU Directive (confirmed in *CLECE SA v Maria Socorro Martin Valor and Ayuntamiento de Cobisa* [2011] IRLR 251). Examples of a service provision that would be affected by TUPE include re-tendering, contracting-out/outsourcing, and contracting-in/in-sourcing (*Hunt v Storm Communications, Wild Card Public Relations and Brown Brothers Wines* [2007] UKEAT/2702456/06). Whether contracting out of services is a 'service provision' for the purposes of TUPE Regulation 3(1)(b) is a matter of law, while the identification of the actual activities are a matter of fact (*Ward Hadaway Solicitors v Capsticks Solicitors LLP* [2010] UKEAT/0471/09/SM).

A service transfer may apply to the assignment of a lease of a commercial property, but this does not naturally follow that all such transfers will invoke TUPE. There must also be an economic entity retaining its identity (incorporating an 'organised grouping' of employees) which is transferred with the lease for TUPE to apply (see *LOM Management v Sweeney* [2012] UKEATS/0058/11/BI).

Organised grouping

For the purposes of a service provision change invoking TUPE, employees are protected where they are an 'organised grouping' of employees. These employees must be situated in the UK and the group must have its principal purpose of carrying out the activities of the client. The 'grouping' may be just one employee, but simply working on a contract does not provide a qualification to protection. Even where an individual is employed for 100 per cent of their time working for a single client, this will not necessarily mean that they are assigned to an organised grouping of employees to establish a transfer for the purposes of the Regulations.

Hence there must be a deliberate act of putting the group of employees together to work for the client.

KEY CASE ANALYSIS: *Seawell v Ceva* **[2012] UKEATS/0034/11/BI**

Background

- The claimant had been employed by Ceva, a company which provided logistics for Seawell.
- Seawell terminated this arrangement with Ceva and brought the service back in-house.
- The claimant had worked 100 per cent of his time at Ceva on the Seawell contract (and other employees had worked less than 100 per cent of their time on the contract but, frequently, substantial amounts of time).
- On the transfer of the service, the claimant considered himself transferred to Seawell.

Principle established

- The EAT disagreed with the employment tribunal's finding that the claimant was an 'organised grouping' of employees.
- The EAT held that in order to satisfy the requirements of an 'organised grouping' there had to be a deliberate/conscious act of organising a group to fulfil the work for the client. This does not occur as a matter of 'happenstance'.
- In this case, there was no such deliberate act and therefore the claimant was not an 'organised grouping' to invoke a TUPE transfer.

Economic, Technical or Organisational defence

As stated above, where a buyer purchases a business that is either failing or where they believe the business could be better run, this will involve either employees being dismissed, or changes (variation) to the contracts of employment following the transfer. While such action is contrary to TUPE protection, a buyer must be able to make changes to the business in its best interests (including, perhaps, those of shareholders). The buyer of a business may make changes to contracts, including dismissals, where this action is part of an **Economic, Technical or Organisational (ETO) reason**. An ETO reason stops what would otherwise be an automatically unfair dismissal, it merely means that an affected employee could be dismissed for redundancy or some other substantial reason. Both of these potentially fair reasons for dismissal are subject to ERA 1996 s. 98(4) requiring the employer to have acted reasonably.

Key Definition: Economic, Technical or Organisational (ETO) reason

Following a transfer of an undertaking regulated by the Transfer of Undertakings (Protection of Employment) Regulations 2006, where an employee is dismissed or where their terms and conditions have been altered (and connected to the transfer), such action may be justified by the employer due to an economic, technical or organisational reason.

Examples of ETO reasons are:

- Economic: the business needs to reduce its overheads due to a reduction in orders and this means that some employees are no longer required.
- Technical: new technology is to be used in the business and the transferring employees do not have the required skills.
- Organisational: where a business already has (for example) an operations director and the business being purchased has an operations director. There would be no organisational need for two people to occupy this one role.

REMEDIES

Where an employee has been dismissed in contravention of TUPE, the remedies for unfair dismissal are available. In *Manchester College v Hazel* [2012] UKEAT/0642/11/RN, following the tribunal and EAT's finding of automatically unfair dismissal, the EAT agreed that the appropriate remedy was re-engagement on newly imposed contracts, but on the old terms before the transfer of the contract of employment.

Compensation payments are also made on the same basis as for unfair dismissal (see Chapter 8). Where a settlement payment has been made prior to the claimant's case being heard at the tribunal, this will reduce any compensatory award made as required by ERA 1996 s. 123 (see *Optimum Group Services PLC v Muir* [2012] UKEATS/0036/12/BI).

EMPLOYEE RELATIONS: INFORMATION AND CONSULTATION

Due to the significance of a transfer of a business or possible redundancies, and the uncertainty this can create through rumours in the workplace, it is wise for an employer to disclose this information in as timely a manner as possible. This is part of good industrial relations and helps to maintain trust between the employer and the workforce. Beyond the benefits this provides for the relationship between the parties, there is also a legal obligation to consult on such changes. Note the important wording here – it is a consultation process whereby the employer passes on the relevant information, it does not require the employer to negotiate on the proposed sale or redundancies.

Transfer consultation

An employer must consult with a representative(s) of the employees or their recognised trade union about the transfer by the employer and any proposed action(s) by the new employer that will affect the workforce (*Alamo v Tucker* [2003] IRLR 266). The information to be provided before the transfer should, at the very least, contain the following:

- when and how the transfer will happen;
- the measures that the new employer is considering, such as redundancies, relocation, and changes to terms and conditions.

Redundancy consultation

To ensure, as far as is possible, that employers are able to make tough business decisions such as closing parts of the operation, while similarly protecting employees from unfairness in the redundancy selection process, the law has developed mechanisms to promote transparency of decision-making. Part of this movement was to require employers who were contemplating (not restricted to those planning) to make collective redundancies to consult (but not negotiate) with a recognised trade union or other employee representative group (Trade Union and Labour Relations (Consolidation) Act (TULR(C)A) 1992 ss. 188–198).

Section 188(1A) outlines the requirements to consult. Where collective redundancies are being considered (and for the purposes of a consistent interpretation with EU law this is the employer's intention to terminate the contracts rather than the actual termination (*Junk v Kuhnel* [2005] IRLR 310)), the following information must be provided:

- The reason for the redundancies, the numbers of employees involved, ways in which these can be avoided/minimised, how the selection process will work, how redundancy payments will be calculated, and any limitation techniques the employer can provide such as retaining or re-deployment.

The employer will then respond to any questions/representations made.

Prior to any collective redundancy consultation, the employer must notify the Insolvency Service Redundancy Payments Service. Failure to make the required notification is a criminal offence and can lead to a maximum £5,000 fine. Further, an employer's failure to consult can lead to compensation being awarded of 8 weeks' pay for each employee affected.

Where collective redundancies are being considered, the law as of 6 April 2013 (TULR(C)A 1992 (Amendment) Order 2013 SI 763/2013) requires the employer to consult at least 30 days before any dismissals take effect where between 20–99 redundancies are planned; and a 45-day minimum consultation period where 100 or more redundancies are planned. Employees to be included in the calculation include those engaged on a fixed-term contract that is to be terminated earlier than that identified in the contract. Individuals engaged on a fixed-term contract whose contract would end before or on the date of the redundancy do not need to be included. Breach of these requirements will lead to subsequent redundancies being held as unfair.

A recent decision by the EAT in *USDAW v WW Realisation Ltd* [2013] ET/3201156/10 has profound effects for redundancy consultation. The consultation period requirement before proposed redundancies take effect is dependent on the number of employees involved (TULR(C)A 1992 s. 188). Section 188 calculates the number of employees (whether between 20–99 or greater than 100) on the basis of those 'at one establishment'. For large employers with various establishments throughout the country this benefited employers as redundancies involving fewer than 20 or between 20–99 employees at each establishment resulted in no or a lesser consultation period being applied. However, in *USDAW*, the EAT had to interpret s. 188 in accordance with the European Collective Redundancies Directive (which required the words 'at one establishment' to be disregarded) and the result was that the statutory duty to consult applies to any employer where they are proposing to make redundant (in total) 20 or more employees, regardless of the particular (separate) establishments at which they work.

> ### On-the-spot question
>
> **?** Given this new development, and where, as is likely to be the case with larger employers who may have redundancies among several locations (possibly in a piecemeal fashion), how easy will it be for the employer to identify when the obligation for consultation applies?

A 'special circumstances' defence is available for employer's who fail to comply with the obligation to consult where it was not reasonably practicable for them to do so (*Clarks of Hove Ltd v Bakers' Union* [1978] IRLR 366). However, this does not mean that failing to comply with the minimum consultation period removes the employer's duty to consult at all. In *Shanahan Engineering v Unite the Union* [2010] UKEAT/0411/09 the EAT held that the employer could have consulted over a 2–3 day period and as they failed to do so, **protective awards** were ordered.

> ### Key Definition: Protective award
>
> A 'protective award' is an award of compensation (ordered by the employment tribunal) to employees who have (collectively) been made redundant, where the employer has failed to consult with their representative/trade union as required by Trade Union and Labour Relations (Consolidation) Act 1992 s. 188.

CHANGES TO THE LAW

The government has been introducing many changes to employment law and continues to do so. Those that have already come into force have been included, but some are still subject to passage through parliament. In relation to TUPE, the government has begun a consultation process on whether the service provision element of the law should be retained or repealed. Given the significance of this issue, ensure that you refer to the companion website for any updates.

CONCLUSION

Redundancy and TUPE are of vital importance in protecting the rights of employees while also identifying specific procedures an employer must follow if they are not to be subject to a claim (and given that these rights often affect more than one employee, multiple claims based on the same error by the employer are quite possible). Protection of these rights is also part of a wider concept of ensuring good industrial relations between the owners/managers of a business and the workforce. Industrial relations is the subject matter of the next chapter.

FURTHER READING

Creighton-Selvay, K. (2013) 'Pre-packed Administrations: An Empirical Social Rights Analysis', *Industrial Law Journal*, Vol. 42, No. 2, p. 85.
The article presents an interesting account of the limitations of the TUPE law in relation to modern corporate restructuring, and presents data advancing an alternative approach.

McMullen, J. (2012) 'Service Provision Change Under TUPE: Not Quite What We Thought', *Industrial Law Journal*, Vol. 41, No. 4, p. 471.
A timely article considering the differing approaches taken by domestic and EU law in relation to the service provision element of TUPE and the Acquired Rights Directive.

McMullen, J. (2006) 'An Analysis of the Transfer of Undertakings (Protection of Employment) Regulations 2006', *Industrial Law Journal*, Vol. 35, No. 2, p. 113.
An analysis of the changes between the TUPE regulations 1981 and 2006 and the advancement of individuals' rights when a business is transferred.

Wynn-Evans, C. (2013) 'In Defence of Service Provision Changes?', *Industrial Law Journal*, Vol. 42, No. 2, p. 152.
A critical analysis of the governmental proposals to end the service provision element of TUPE, and the potential problems this would cause in relation to employment protection and competition.

Chapter 10
Industrial action

LEARNING OUTCOMES

Having read this chapter you should be in a position to:

- identify the distinction between official and unofficial industrial action;
- explain the reason for the existence of industrial action and how it assists the weaker party (such as an individual) to compel a more powerful party (such as an employer) to negotiate on terms and conditions of work;
- explain the process of immunity from liability for trade unions and individuals when conducting official industrial action;
- identify the key concept of the 'golden formula' and its implications when contemplating taking industrial action;
- explain the process and requirements of holding a lawful ballot;
- identify the areas of potential liability of trade unions and individuals, and be able to explain the powers available to employers to protect them when faced with industrial action.

MIND MAP

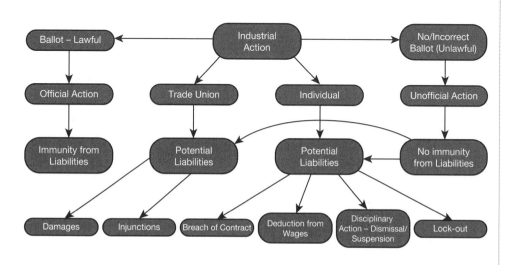

INTRODUCTION

Individuals have the right to join a trade union and to take part in the activities of trade unions. It should also be borne in mind when considering trade union membership that the old concept, fostered particularly in the 1970s and 80s, of trade unions being aggressive and militant and working against an employer's best interests is very rarely the case in the modern era. Most trade unions now actively seek to engage positively with the employer, to provide assistance and advice wherever possible, and have a much better cooperative relationship with their members and the employer than perhaps the negative connotation of the term 'trade union' would suggest.

EMPLOYER ACTION AGAINST TRADE UNION MEMBERSHIP

The dismissal of an employee for the reason of his or her trade union membership, or because he or she intended to join a trade union, or where the dismissal is connected to his or her participation in the activities of the trade union is automatically unfair (TULR(C)A 1992, s. 154).

It is an automatically unfair reason to dismiss an employee because of their membership (or non-membership) of a trade union. It is also unfair not to employ an individual because of trade union membership. However, in *Miller v Interserve Industrial Services Ltd* [2012] UKEAT/0244/12, the EAT held that this does not mean that there are no exceptions to this general rule. In *Miller*, an employer refused to employ three individuals whom a trade union official had strongly urged the employer to recruit. Section 137(1) of TULR(C)A 1992 prevents an employer's refusal to employ because of trade union membership, but it was held that the employer felt bullied by the official and did not wish to be dictated to regarding his recruitment exercises. The EAT held that it was simply a case of the affected individuals being caught in the 'crossfire' between the employer and the trade union, although it did further remark that such reasons put forward by an employer would be scrutinised to ensure that this was the real reason for the refusal to employ.

INDUSTRIAL ACTION

Industrial action is a mechanism whereby employees can exert power over the employer to participate in negotiations regarding, for example, terms and conditions at work. At the outset it is worth remembering that in the United Kingdom, most individuals at work have relatively little power compared with the employer. The employer is the person who will set the terms and conditions of the contract, they will largely determine the employment status of the individual, and ultimately the employer has the power to terminate the contract (although of course individuals may choose to resign). Individuals, acting individually, have little power, but when they work collectively, they have the power to withdraw their labour, cause inconvenience to their employer, and through such action, do have certain powers to ensure an employer will negotiate with them and/or their representatives. Be aware that there is no official legal definition of industrial action. What we have are examples from case law and through these we see the following actions:

* refusal to carry out lawful and reasonable instructions;
* taking part in strike action and picketing;
* a collective withdrawal of labour;
* refusal to undertake all partial duties (serve the employer faithfully);
* actions short of full withdrawal of labour, for example, 'work to rule' and adopting a 'go slow' policy.

Key Definition: Official industrial action

Remember the disclaimer above about official definitions of industrial action. However, industrial action involves a concerted action against the employer's interests, aimed at 'encouraging' the employer to negotiate to achieve a particular objective, which need not necessarily involve a breach of contract.

It is also important to remember that there is no positive right to strike and all that has been established is for a series of immunities from liability which shield or protect the trade union, strike organisers, and the individuals participating in **'official' industrial action**. The most significant piece of legislation regarding industrial action is the Trade Union and Labour Relations (Consolidation) Act (TULR(C)A) 1992. It is very important that you understand this piece of legislation and refer to your statute books for precise authority.

Key Definition: Unofficial industrial action

Unofficial industrial action, including strike action, is unofficial where it is unauthorised or not endorsed by the participants' trade union or where it has been repudiated by it. Hence, the organisers of the action are acting outside the union's rules or in defiance of its instruction.

On-the-spot question

? Compare the rights of individuals in the United Kingdom to participate in strike action compared with the rights given to similar workers in countries including France and Italy. Why do you think the UK is so restrictive and do you believe this approach benefits workers, employers, and/or the economy?

Procedures for calling industrial action

The TULR(C)A 1992 identifies strict criteria by which the parties mentioned above will gain protection against liability when involved in industrial action. These must be followed because the consequences, particularly for trade unions, can be devastating when they are involved in **unofficial industrial action**.

Prior to any call to industrial action, the trade union will seek immunity, provided through TULR(C)A 1992, s. 219. These provisions must be strictly adhered to or the trade union exposes itself to financial penalties that could be devastating. The requirements are as follows (see TULR(C)A 1992, ss. 226–35):

- The majority of union members who can be called upon to take industrial action must have voted in support of that action through a properly conducted ballot.
- The ballot is required in respect of an act 'done by a trade union' and can be authorised (that is agreed prior) or endorsed (agreed afterwards).
- The act of authorisation or endorsement will be taken as such whereby the action is from any person who is empowered by the rules of the trade union to do so (e.g. a trade union official); the principal executive committee or the president; or any other committee of the union or official (TULR(C)A 1992, 20(2)).
- There must be a separate ballot for each workplace (TULR(C)A 1992, ss. 228(1) and 228A) subject to the exceptions contained in the Act).
- The ballot paper must ask whether the voter is prepared to take part in, or to continue to take part in, a strike, to which the answer must be 'yes' or 'no'.
- The ballot paper must identify the person(s) authorised to call upon members to take industrial action if the vote permits (TULR(C)A 1992, s. 20(2)).
- The ballot paper must identify the independent scrutineer where required under (TULR(C)A 1992, 20(2)).
- A copy of the ballot paper must be provided to the employer.
- The ballot must be a secret, postal ballot (TULR(C)A 1992, ss. 227, 230, 232A and 232B).
- Where the vote has been in favour of industrial action, the action must be called within four weeks beginning on the date of the ballot (TULR(C)A 1992, s. 234(1)).

This period may be extended up to eight weeks where the trade union and the employer agree.

- The union is required to give the employer seven days written notice of any industrial action based on the ballot result. This requirement of notice applies to intermittent action such as one-day strikes.
- As soon as is reasonably practicable after a ballot, the trade union shall take such steps as are reasonably necessary to ensure that the members eligible to vote are informed of the number of votes cast; the number of individuals answering yes and no; and the number of spoilt ballot papers (TULR(C)A 1992, s. 213).

Further, information to which an employer is entitled to receive includes:

- notice of the union's intention to hold a ballot (and details of those entitled to vote, and the voting procedures);
- a sample copy of the paper – to identify the questions asked; and
- details of the results given to the members and the report provided to the scrutineer.

The requirements of holding a lawful ballot are quite onerous, but in the 2010 case, the Court of Appeal provided some latitude to trades unions.

KEY CASE ANALYSIS: *British Airways plc v Unite the Union* [2010] EWCA Civ 669

Background

- The claimants sought an injunction to prevent the union from seeking to induce employees to breach their contract through unlawful industrial action.
- The claimant argued that the union had failed to comply with TULR(C)A 1992, s. 231 regarding information that the union members should have received with regards to the results of the ballot.
- Information had been provided in a variety of ways including a website and notice boards.
- The claimant further argued that the union did not disseminate information about the votes cast and any spoiled papers.

Principle established

- The Court of Appeal held that the concept of 'reasonableness' established in s. 231 resulted in the trade union not having to prove that every eligible member of the union was personally sent the report.
- Lady Justice Smith further commented that the requirements had not been breached in anything other than a minor way and they should not invalidate the ballot or its results.

Sanctions against individuals involved in industrial action

There exist different sanctions depending on whether the individual has been involved in official or unofficial industrial action. Do remember however, that individuals involved in strike action do not break their continuity of service (necessary for claims involving unfair dismissal and redundancy, etc.) where the individual returns to work after the strike. It will suspend the qualifying period during the action and this must be taken into account (regarding the number of days involved in strike action) when identifying employment rights and their qualifying periods.

Breach of contract

It is important that individuals who breach the contract of employment, particularly when involved with industrial action, are not subject to punitive sanctions. This means that when awarding damages, courts must be mindful of the financial power of the employer compared with the limitations of the financial power of the individual. In previous cases, employers attempted to recover damages for the loss of output resulting from individuals' involvement in strike action. This would have been economically debilitating for individuals who would not have had the required financial resources to satisfy such a claim. Indeed, in *National Coal Board v Galley* [1958] 1 All ER 91 the court recognised this fact and while it upheld the employer's legal right to claim for losses against the striking employee, this was reduced to the cost of providing a substitute (another employee doing the work) rather than for the loss of output experienced by the employer.

Where the employer does accept the industrial action, a deduction of wages is possible in accordance with the contract – see *Sim v Rotherham Metropolitan Borough Council* [1986] IRLR 391 and what was known as the 'equitable set-off' deduction. Where the employer does not accept the industrial action, the consequences can be seen below.

Deduction from wages

The House of Lords established the general rule in the case *Miles v Wakefield Metropolitan District Council* [1987] IRLR 193 of the principle of 'no pay for no work'. Where an individual is involved in industrial action the employer does not have to pay wages, as no work is being performed under the general mutual obligations between the parties, and further, in the following case the Court of Appeal established the state of law regarding 'partial' industrial action: where deductions are made on the basis of the employer accepting the industrial action, they should be reasonable, clearly identified, and it is good practice to warn employees in advance of any industrial action, of this consequence, and to allow employees who wish to distance themselves from industrial action to do so.

KEY CASE ANALYSIS: *Wiluszynski v Tower Hamlets LBC* [1989] IRLR 258

Background

- The claimant employee was a housing officer, and a member of the trade union involved in industrial action where he was to refuse to answer enquiries from liberal/SDP controlled council members.
- This was a very minor part of his job which took up approximately three hours of work over a five-week period.
- The employer had warned the claimant that no payment would be made if this industrial action was taken.
- The claimant participated in the industrial action and, when no payment of wages was made, claimed the balance of the wages owed on the basis of (among others) his substantial performance.

Principle established

- The employee's claim for wages on a proportional basis failed.
- Even though the employer benefited from the work undertaken by the employee, the employer did not direct him in the work, the employer did not accept the work being performed, and therefore the employee was entitled to no wages.
- Employers do not have to accept industrial action. Where they do not accept the action, they do not have to pay any (full, proportional/pro rata) wages.

Disciplinary action

Chapters 7 and 8 have dealt with situations involving dismissals and disciplinary action for breach of contract. While a withdrawal of labour can involve a refusal to obey a lawful order or constitute acting in bad faith, the 'general' contractual principles for the consequences of the breach are not particularly appropriate in cases of industrial action, due in part to the statutory protections and obligations on the parties.

Dismissal

The general rule is that dismissal of individuals involved in unofficial strikes is fair on the basis that employment tribunals have no jurisdiction to hear such cases. Therefore the individual has nowhere to have their claim heard.

In relation to those individuals taking part in official strike action, this raises the issue or immunities from sanctions as the trade union will have complied with the requirements of TULR(C)A 1992. This is sometimes referred to as 'protected action' as it provides individuals with limited protection against dismissal when taking part in industrial action. Had there been no such protection available, the entire benefit for individuals with limited power against a much more powerful employer would have been lost. Industrial action enables the weaker party to require the more powerful party to negotiate and take their requests seriously.

TULR(C)A 1992, s. 238A protects an employee who has taken part in, or was taking part in, **protected industrial action**, and who was dismissed as a consequence of this action. Where the dismissal has taken place within 12 weeks of the employee starting the industrial action, the employee may claim unfair dismissal at an employment tribunal. The dismissal may also be unfair where the 12-week period has passed, but the employer had not taken reasonable steps to resolve the dispute.

Key Definition: Protected industrial action

The term which applies to official industrial action where the trade union has immunity from liability under TULR(C)A 1992, s. 219.

Where protection through TULR(C)A 1992, s. 238A is not available, an employee who was dismissed for taking part in official industrial action will generally not be able to claim unfair dismissal unless the employer has selectively chosen to dismiss employees involved in industrial action or had offered such persons re-engagement within three months of the date of dismissal (TULR(C)A 1992, s. 238).

Remember, the TULR(C)A 1992 is a statutory measure and protects against unfair dismissal – or at the very least provides the individual with the rights to claim unfair dismissal when the employer acts in breach of the legislation. At common law, the employer is entitled to dismiss an individual who acts in breach of contract, and strike action will almost certainly be held as a repudiatory breach of contract. This allows summary dismissal without pay.

Suspension

In the event of industrial action, an employer may wish to consider suspending the individual(s) involved, particularly where the industrial action has involved separate, disciplinary offences. However, suspension must be provided with full pay unless the contract of employment specifically allows for suspension without pay. This is a difficult area of law and dismissal or some other sanction may be more appropriate.

Lock-out

An employer may seek to close or to cease operations completely at a workplace where a group of individuals have taken strike action. This prevents any of those individuals from attending work. This is a somewhat unusual disciplinary measure as it prevents employees who were not involved in the strike from attending work, and it opens the employer to the possibility of a breach of contract claim by such affected individuals.

Sanctions against trade union/organisers involved in industrial action

Trade unions gain protection where they require their members to take part in official industrial action. Where the action is unofficial, this exposes the unions to potentially large financial sanctions, particularly in the law of torts (known as the 'economic torts'). The courts have developed several torts over the years and the main torts are:

Inducement of breach of contract

Inducement requires an attempt, through pressure or persuasion on a contracting party, to act in breach of the contract. A trade union, for example, will perhaps require its members to take part in industrial action and thereby to breach the contract. The trade union has no contract with the employer, but its actions are inducing one of the parties to the contract to act in breach (see – *Lumley v Gye* [1853] 2 El & Bl 216). This is the main economic tort against trade unions. There are two dimensions to the inducement, direct inducement and indirect inducement:

DIRECT INDUCEMENT

Direct inducement applies where the defendant induces a third party to breach an existing contract. The trade union has not breached the contract, as it is the third party, not the trade union, who has a contract with the claimant, and the claimant will have suffered loss due to this breach. For example, the trade union, through its official, instructs a third party (here it is the employee) to breach the contract by taking strike action against the claimant (the employer) who suffers loss as a result. In order to have committed this tort, there must have been knowledge that the contract was in existence, intention to cause its breach, an actual breach having taken place, and evidence of the union's inducement.

INDIRECT INDUCEMENT

Indirect inducement is where unlawful means are used to render the performance of the contract, by one of the parties, impossible. An example of indirect inducement would be as follows. Company B supplies goods under a commercial contract to Company A. A dispute exists between the employees of Company A with their employer. A worker at Company B is persuaded by a trade union official not to make deliveries to Company A. The result of this action is that the trade union official has directly induced the worker at Company B to break the contract, and has, through unlawful means, indirectly induced the breach of a commercial contract between Company A and Company B (see *DC Thomson v Deakin* [1952] 2 All ER 361).

Note that in the case *OBG v Allan* [2008] 1 AC the House of Lords held that a breach occurs regardless of whether there is direct or indirect inducement. The tort of inducement does not need to be differentiated for liability to be incurred.

Interference with the contract, trade or business

In *Torquay Hotel Co Ltd. v Cousins* [1969] 2 Ch. 106, the Court of Appeal held that persuasion by a trade union, in dispute with the owner of the hotel, with the suppliers of oil (a third party) used in the hotel's central heating system, to breach the contract amounted to interference with performance of the contract and was a tort. This was independent of the contractual relationship between the hotel and the defendant. The House of Lords, in *OBG v Allan* [2008] required that the interference must be brought about through unlawful means, for example, through a breach of statutory duty. Further, the interference is now broadened through the tort of causing loss to interference with a person's business trade and is not restricted to contractual relationships (see *Merkur Island Shipping Corp v Laughton* [1983] 2 AC 570).

Intimidation

The tort exists where a person, through acts including threats of violence or threatening to breach a contract or inducement to breach a contract, causes the other party loss. This tort used to be confined to acts of violence, but was extended to an act of inducement to breach contracts through the House of Lords judgment in *Rookes v Barnard* [1964] 1 All ER 367.

Immunities against sanction

Trade unions obtain (at least a prima facie) immunity against sanction for the various torts above where the action was taken 'in contemplation or furtherance of a trade dispute'. This is part of the wording from TULR(C)A 1992, s. 219 and is known as the 'golden formula'.

Section 219 provides: Protection from certain tort liabilities.

(1) An act done by a person in contemplation or furtherance of a trade dispute is not actionable in tort on the ground only—

(a) that it induces another person to break a contract or interferes or induces another person to interfere with its performance, or

(b) that it consists in his threatening that a contract (whether one to which he is a party or not) will be broken or its performance interfered with, or that he will induce another person to break a contract or interfere with its performance.

Hence, actions taken by a person in contemplation of furtherance of the **trade dispute** will not be actionable in tort only where it induces the other person to break a contract or interferes or induces any other person to interfere with its performance.

Key Definition: Trade dispute

A dispute between an employer and the collective workforce regarding potential conditions of work.

In order to gain protection the industrial action must satisfied the following criteria:

1 The dispute must be between the workers and their employer. Immunity will not be granted where the dispute is between the employer and the workers, workers and workers, or the workers and another employee (so-called secondary industrial action), or trade unions as parties to a dispute (*NWL v Woods* [1979] 1 WLR 1294).

2 There must be a dispute, and this applies even where an employer is willing to agree to the demands of the particular trade union (see TULR(C)A 1992, s. 244(4)).

3 The subject matter of the dispute must be related to one or more of those identified in s. 244(1) – such as the terms of employment, disciplinary measures, membership or non-membership of a trade union.

4 The action must be in contemplation or furtherance of a trade dispute. This means that the person taking the action must honestly believe that it would further the trade dispute and bring it closer to a resolution.

Loss of immunity

Immunity is provided insofar as the golden formula is complied with. Any form of secondary action is not considered lawful and will not gain protection for the union, whether that action is effected through inducement or picketing.

Employers are not permitted to operate a 'closed shop' whereby individuals have to be members of a particular trade union to gain employment.

The action taken by the members on the instruction of the trade union must be considered official trade union action to attract the immunities through the golden formula. This requires that the procedural elements of lawful ballots are complied with.

Powers of trade union members

Where the trade union has instructed its members to take industrial action that is not supported through the holding of a lawful ballot, it loses its immunities. Also, a member, who has been, is likely to be, or was induced to take action on the basis of this instruction has the right to apply to the High Court for an order requiring the union to withdraw its authorisation or endorsement (TULR(C)A 1992, s. 62).

Damages

The Employment Act 1982 established the ability of an employer to sue a trade union in damages for losses associated with unlawful industrial action. The trade union may further be held vicariously liable where industrial action is authorised by it, or endorsed by it, or by those empowered to do so. This provided great leverage to employers in their battles with trade unions. TULR(C)A 1992, s. 22 places limitations on the award of damages, applicable to each claim against the trade union, which Table 10.1 identifies.

Table 10.1 Limitations of the award of damages

Compensation of damages payment	Number of members of the union
£10,000	Union with fewer than 5,000 members
£50,000	Union between 5,000, but fewer than 25,000 members
£125,000	Union with more than 25,000, but fewer than 100,000 members
£250,000	Union has 100,000 or more members

Injunctions

The primary remedy given in cases of breach of contract or torts is a monetary payment called damages. Where such a remedy would not adequately compensate the injured party, the courts have the power to use equitable remedies including injunctions. The requirements of the court to award an injunction is that the conduct of the defendant is causing a level of harm that damages would not, subsequently, compensate, and that the harm being suffered and incurred by the claimant is greater than the harm that would be incurred by the defendants if they were to cease their activities (the 'balance of convenience' test).

The most common form of injunction is a prohibitory injunction, which is a court order compelling the defendant to stop such an action. There also exists a mandatory injunctions, which is a court order compelling the defendant to do something. Finally, and most apt for cases of industrial action, an interim injunction is available through which a court has the power to compel a trade union to cease its industrial action pending a full trial. The House of Lords, in *American Cyanamid Co v Ethicon Ltd* [1975] 2 WLR 316 identified that interim relief can be provided where there is a 'serious issue' to be tried.

On-the-spot question

? Given the tests identified above, do you think it would be particularly difficult for the claimant employer to obtain an interim injunction? Further, what are the potential problems faced by trades unions and individuals when their powers to take industrial action are inhibited in this way? (See *The National Union of Rail, Maritime & Transport Workers v Serco Limited (& others)* [2011] EWCA Civ. 226).

PICKETING

There is no right to picket but rather there is a limited immunity from civil and criminal liability where the action taken complies with TULR(C)A 1992, s. 220(1)(a):

> It shall be lawful for a person in contemplation or furtherance of a trade dispute to attend:
> (a)   at or near his own place of work; or
> (b)   if he is an official of a trade union, at or near the place of work of a member of that union whom he is accompanying and whom he represents, for the purposes only of communicating information or peacefully persuading any person to work or abstain from working.

The restrictions ensure that the pickets may only attend at or near their own workplace (the element of 'near' a workplace relates to those people engaged, for example, on an oil rig, and the individuals' 'own' workplace can encompass more than one venue where the individual is engaged at more than one location). The DBIS has a Code of Practice on Picketing which provides, among many other provisions, that no more than six pickets at a time should occupy the place of work.

Picketing, without the relevant immunity, could result in individuals being held liable for the tort of inducing breach of contract, further there is a possibility of a private nuisance claim for the unlawful interference with an individual's use or enjoyment of their land. The very purpose of picketing is to bring attention to the dispute between the workers and their employer, and to peacefully attempt to persuade others not to cross the picket line. Communicating information for these lawful purposes avoids the tort of nuisance, although there is still a question as to whether without the protection of TULR(C)A 1992, s. 219, picketing itself would amount to a nuisance.

There also exist potential criminal liabilities for picketing, particularly in relation to actions that could amount to a breach of the peace and obstruction of the highway (also a potential public nuisance where an individual suffers special damage over and above that suffered by the rest of the public (see *News Group Newspapers Ltd v Society of Graphical and Allied Trades* [1986] IRLR 227).

CONCLUSION

This concluding chapter has identified some of the major features of industrial action, the requirements imposed on trade unions and individuals participating in this action, their ability to obtain immunities from liability, and the rights, obligations and actions available to employers when faced with the disruption caused through industrial action.

FURTHER READING

Gall, G. (2012) 'Union Recognition in Britain: The End of Legally Induced Voluntarism?', *Industrial Law Journal*, Vol. 41, No. 4, p.407.
An article examining the balance of power in employment relations and its effects for the system of voluntary trade union recognition.

Prassi, J. (2011) 'To Strike, to Serve? Industrial Action at British Airways. *British Airways plc v Unite the Union (Nos 1 and 2)*', *Industrial Law Journal*, Vol. 40, No. 1, p. 82.
An interesting note on the case(s) and the legal issues surrounding the complexity of lawful industrial action when faced with the threat of an employer seeking an injunction restraining such action.

Simpson, B. (2013) 'The Labour Injunction and Industrial Action Ballots', *Industrial Law Journal*, Vol. 42, No. 1, p. 54.
A critique of the judgments concerning balloting requirements needed to qualify for protection against the potential liabilities under the economic torts.

Simpson, B. (2007) 'Economic Tort Liability in Labour Disputes: The Potential Impact of *OBG v Allan*', *Industrial Law Journal*, Vol. 36, No. 4, p. 468.
A case commentary looking at the implications of the *OBG* case and the liability of those involved in organising industrial action for economic torts.

Index